# Cambridge Elements

**Elements in Intercultural Communication**
edited by
Will Baker
*University of Southampton*
Troy McConachy
*University of New South Wales, Australia*
Sonia Morán Panero
*University of Southampton*

# CONSTRAINED MULTILINGUALISM

Marco Santello
*University of Turin*

Shaftesbury Road, Cambridge CB2 8EA, United Kingdom

One Liberty Plaza, 20th Floor, New York, NY 10006, USA

477 Williamstown Road, Port Melbourne, VIC 3207, Australia

314–321, 3rd Floor, Plot 3, Splendor Forum, Jasola District Centre,
New Delhi – 110025, India

Cambridge University Press is part of Cambridge University Press & Assessment, a department of the University of Cambridge.

We share the University's mission to contribute to society through the pursuit of education, learning and research at the highest international levels of excellence.

www.cambridge.org
Information on this title: www.cambridge.org/9781009650601

DOI: 10.1017/9781009650557

© Marco Santello 2026

This publication is in copyright. Subject to statutory exception and to the provisions of relevant collective licensing agreements, no reproduction of any part may take place without the written permission of Cambridge University Press & Assessment.

When citing this work, please include a reference to the DOI 10.1017/9781009650557

First published 2026

*A catalogue record for this publication is available from the British Library*

*A Cataloging-in-Publication data record for this Element is available from the Library of Congress*

ISBN 978-1-009-65060-1 Hardback
ISBN 978-1-009-65059-5 Paperback
ISSN 2752-5589 (online)
ISSN 2752-5570 (print)

Cambridge University Press & Assessment has no responsibility for the persistence or accuracy of URLs for external or third-party internet websites referred to in this publication and does not guarantee that any content on such websites is, or will remain, accurate or appropriate.

For EU product safety concerns, contact us at Calle de José Abascal, 56, 1°, 28003 Madrid, Spain, or email eugpsr@cambridge.org

# Constrained Multilingualism

Elements in Intercultural Communication

DOI: 10.1017/9781009650557
First published online: March 2026

---

Marco Santello
*University of Turin*

Author for correspondence: Marco Santello, marco.santello@unito.it

**Abstract:** This Element highlights the role of constraints in shaping multilingualism. It discusses their conceptualisation, starting from Michel de Certeau's view of action in everyday life, and operationalisation for the study of migrants. The results of the research conducted among Gambian migrants in Italy show not only constraints but also the tactics to inhabit them, as well as non-language-related aspects, for example suffering, which are grouped into five clusters. These are (1) lack of support; (2) limited interaction in the 'local' language; (3) immigration status in conjunction with life events; (4) others' behaviour; and (5) other concerns and suffering. The conclusion presents a discussion on the wider significance of what incorporating constraints means for our understanding of multilingualism and migration, including policy implications, and for intercultural communication research.

This Element also has a video abstract:
www.cambridge.org/EIIC_Santello_abstract

**Keywords:** multilingualism, constraints, migration, multilingual theory, multilingual practices

© Marco Santello 2026

ISBNs: 9781009650601 (HB), 9781009650595 (PB), 9781009650557 (OC)
ISSNs: 2752-5589 (online), 2752-5570 (print)

# Contents

1 Introduction     1

2 Conceptualising and Operationalising Constraints     3

3 Unearthing Constraints among Multilingual Migrants     14

4 Significance of Constrained Multilingualism for the Understanding of Migration     36

Appendix     44

References     45

## 1 Introduction

The central argument of this Element is that constraints are implicated in multilingualism in ways that have not been fully accounted for. I will argue that constraints, rather than functioning merely as a blockage for multilingualism, are inhabited through tactics that contribute to the shaping of multilingualism itself. Constraints are intended as circumstances and doing over which one, in this case migrants, does not exercise full control, following Michel de Certeau (1990). I will try to show that if we allow the space to look at constraints that are not *ipso facto* overcome – especially not overcome by language practices – multilingualism can emerge more starkly as it relates to the unchosen circumstances which are present in many lives, including those of migrants. In the examples from migrants in Italy that I will present, it will be clear that some constraints limit their ability to progress in the way these migrants envisage, while others perhaps do, but are not lived out as impediments to communication, and others still are, astonishingly, welcomed as opportunities. This Element therefore somehow follows onto recent scholarship in applied-sociolinguistics that has highlighted the hitherto under-researched value of incompetence (Canagarajah 2022), precariousness (Dovchin et al. 2024), and immobility (De Fina & Mazzaferro 2022) for an understanding of language, while focusing more specifically on multilingualism and communication among migrants. It explores their lived experience with language as it emerges through rapport with the researcher; it is also thanks to the exchange with the researcher (me), progressively exposing his vulnerability that this research unfolds, so that things that do not go according to plan are allowed into and nurture the data.

This framework for understanding multilingualism stems from more general social theory that looks at action in everyday life as intertwined with constraints where people's actions can be tactical, in the sense that they are creative and proactive within a space of action, while not necessarily being transformative at a larger scale. This was the idea that de Certeau (1990) put forward in his renowned work on the invention of everyday life, which, instead of highlighting structure/agency dynamics, sought to understand the tactical nature of the action of the weak in the field of the strong in a different way. As I will explain in Section 2, according to him, there is a space of action carved out in people's daily life that is inhabited creatively within constraints. The aim of this Element, therefore, is to look at how constraints can be theorised, operationalised, and, most importantly, how multilingualism emerges because (rather than in spite) of them. It will be clear that in no way can migrants be seen as passive individuals who simply accept acquiescently what is given. Rather, they are active within a space of action as well as when considering ways in which certain constraints can be overcome.

The Element, which uses material derived from my theoretical and empirical engagement with multilingualism over the past few years (Santello 2022, 2025a, 2025b, 2025c), intends to outline a manner of relating to language in migratory settings that reveals the role of constraints for multilingualism itself, considering again that not overcoming constraints is a common occurrence, and that their persistence can be seen as more than an impediment to creativity. In this sense, this Element, while banking on long-standing theoretical advancements and very recent interpretations of communication and multilingualism, which will be discussed in detail, is in fact a first foray into constrained multilingualism. More broadly, with this research, I seek to identify and explain better what is at work among migrants who are not in full control of circumstances and doing in various ways, which is something I have also experienced in my own life in four countries.

The understanding of language use in migratory settings has been deemed a key topic in intercultural communication for some time now, so much so that the International Association for Languages and Intercultural Communication (IALIC) conference, held in 2024 in Bordeaux, France, had plurilingualism as its central theme. Attention to issues of language and migration has sparked interest in narrative accounts (Ladegaard 2023) and multilingualism in its many forms (Phipps 2019), including new work on vulnerability and multilingualism in research with migrants (Ganassin et al. 2024). This Element, as I will discuss more extensively in the concluding section, speaks to the body of research that looks at intercultural communication as multilingual communication in migratory settings (Piller 2025), showing a side of intercultural communication that revolves around the experience of migrants who are often neglected in scholarly research in the field.

The Element is structured as follows. After this introduction I start with a discussion of how constrained multilingualism can be visualised, based on the questioning of boundary transcendence as the hallmark of multilingualism, aided by Michel de Certeau's understanding of action in everyday life (2.1). The second part of the section (2.2) explains the ways in which constraints can be operationalised so that they emerge in linguistic data. It presents my ethnography among Gambian migrants in Padua, Italy and, in doing so, it highlights the productivity of studying these phenomena through rapport-in-talk, where the exchanges between researcher and participants are key for the identification of the dynamics under study. As previously stated, this encompasses also exposing the researcher's vulnerability, which stems from an enhanced appreciation that 'who we are and who we become in a research setting' (Warriner et al. 2019b, p. 8) has relevance for what unfolds on the ground, for example, when the researcher himself shares difficult personal experiences as a migrant and gets listened to. I will also explain how stance-taking and socio-pragmatics are employed in the analysis.

In Section 3, I present data that provide evidence of what putting constraints and multilingualism in the same equation can show, giving prominence to migrants' experiences as told in interaction. Studying constrained multilingualism means necessarily explaining how constraints are inhabited, for example, through language-related tactics, so I will show how this inhabiting can happen. In other words, finding out constraints means also finding out the space of action individuals have and what they can or cannot do within it. In the sections, I identify four clusters of constraints, namely lack of support (3.1), limited interaction in the 'local' language (3.2), immigration status in conjunction with life events (3.3), and others' behaviour (3.4), followed by Section 3.5 titled 'More than language-related constraints: other concerns and suffering'. The Element concludes with a discussion of what can be understood about migration by studying constrained multilingualism among migrants, where I will also elaborate on the implications of this type of work for intercultural communication research at large (Section 4).

## 2 Conceptualising and Operationalising Constraints

### 2.1 Conceptualising Constraints

There is a whole body of studies that focuses on how migrants interact in a new sociolinguistic environment and, in recent years, increasing attention has been devoted to the resourcefulness of migrants in using their repertoire to make meaning.[1] In fact, the study of language and migration has shown (1) multilingual language practices that denote the resourcefulness of migrants, and (2) structural inequalities that prevent migrants from using their resources freely.

The first group of studies often takes an ethnographic approach and tends to highlight aspects such as fluidity and transcendence of boundaries. This is the case of a city market in England where, when customers and sellers do not have much in common in terms of linguistic history, different ways to make meaning, including gesturing, are employed in commercial transactions (Blackledge & Creese 2017). In other settings, practices other than standard norms are brought to the fore; for example, explaining that in non-Western multilingual societies

---

[1] This section is based largely on Santello (2022, 2025b). To a lesser extent it also draws from Santello (2025a, 2025c). All these works, published as Gold Open Access articles, have been here alternately paraphrased, re-used with the same wording, revised and/or recombined for the purpose of this Element.

communication and negotiation rather than monolingual-like competence are key (Canagarajah & Wurr 2011). In summative accounts of the literature, these types of language use are described as 'locally-occasioned language that is liable in certain circumstances to attract censure informed by dominant monolingual or regulated bilingual (keep-languages-separate) ideologies' (Baynham & Lee 2019, p. 30). They are described as grassroots practices where boundary transcendence is related to creativity (Santello 2022).

The second strand of research has highlighted aspects like injustice (Piller 2016), structural inequalities (Tupas 2015, 2024), discrimination (Dovchin 2022), and immobility (De Fina & Mazzaferro 2022). Taking an approach that draws heavily on social sciences at large, these have noted that migrants are subject to processes they can only partly control. For example, Gal (2006) discusses how German speakers in Hungary and Hungarian speakers in Austria can face ridicule when crossing borders, and Lippi-Green (2012) has stressed the negative impact that accent evaluation can have on speakers. Studies have focused on specific settings such as the workplace, where there might be a 'covert expectation to assimilate linguistically in order to be seen as legitimate professionals' (Harrison 2013, p. 198), or politics, where potential candidates may suffer from large unconscious bias against L2 speakers, therefore limiting their likelihood to run for office (Bonotti & Willoughby 2023).

To be sure, both of these discursive poles have been subject to a good degree of scrutiny and problematisation. Scholars such as Prinsloo (2024) question attributing superior intrinsic value to fluid language practices alone, pointing to both fluid and fixed language practices in society. Drawing on Silverstein (2017), he highlights that, for instance, using a standard language variety can be linked to linguistic creativity, implying therefore that the fixity that characterises certain language practices can also be used in creative ways. May (2022), providing a more general critique of deconstructivism in sociolinguistics, also warns against an excessive focus on individualism and the hybridisation of linguistic practices, arguing that it is important not to underplay the reality that access to standardised varieties plays a role for many language users. By contrast, agency has been identified in how migrants handle top-heavy societal problems that make them victims of injustice. For example, Bucholtz, Casillas, & Lee (2019) have described how young people in California can challenge conditions of injustice linked to their languages of heritage through activism by advocating for the use of Spanish in a commencement speech, thus showing that multilinguals themselves can be involved in change.

In spite of these problematisations, there is a tendency in the field to establish a dichotomy whereby language is creative at the micro-level and constrained at a higher level (Blommaert 2005, p. 125). Rather, Gramling (2021) has questioned the tendency to insist on either powerful macro-social forces that affect languages or unbridled language use at the grassroots level. He wishes for greater interdisciplinary insights and a rethinking of multilingualism as a praxis under pressure. Dovchin (2025a) has contended that playfulness and precarity do not have to be seen as opposite ends in translingualism research, and other scholars have talked about the need to complement approaches that focus on macro-social workings, that is, larger social processes, with less large-scale elements that can also function as constraints (Canagarajah 2022, 2023), for example, in daily mundane interactions. In other words, there is room for research looking at constraints from a variety of perspectives, also conceding that developing linguistically does not necessarily mean breaking free from the undesired. One could question, for instance, if behaving multilingually is primarily about going against rigid language practices that speakers do not want to resort to. In this sense, scholars are starting to assess more systematically the possibility that there could also be value in multilingual practices that operate within constraints rather than going beyond them (Santello 2022). This could revisit the assumption around transcendence of boundaries as the touchstone of multilingualism, giving an enhanced consideration of what it means to operate linguistically – and possibly creatively – within something given, in line with Deumert's (2018) view that expressivity in everyday life does not have to be thought of as automatically implying disruption.

To understand the role of constraints in everyday life, I find it useful to look at the work of Michel de Certeau (1990), whose writings illuminate key societal processes. In looking at them, de Certeau emphasises the relevance of production and consumption. He shows that the activities that are valued in society are usually those that have a function that can be ascertained and classified, and that contribute to some form of production. Similarly, he shows that individuals and groups are meant to be consumers of products, and their actions are often inscribed in exchanges. To put it in another way, according to him, society is affected by functionalism, which means that often what counts is what serves a specific identifiable purpose. In this context, de Certeau stresses the centrality of what he calls 'strategies'. These are ways of doing that establish a dynamic whereby an individual or a group exerts control. Strategies have the role of controlling activities so that they are manageable and can serve their function well; to do so, people that use strategies must have an overview of what occurs and can put in place plans that can encompass and manage what is seen. Control of a place, for instance, can be exerted by strategies such as mapping that describe it in detail so that parts that are not used can be identified and dealt with.

However, de Certeau finds it unacceptable to consider people who do not engage in strategies as passive consumers incapable of doing anything beyond what is imposed on them. Some activities, while based on elements that are not fully chosen, actively re-use what is given. Think of cooking, for example: an individual does not cook in a vacuum or completely evade what surrounds him or her. There are recipes, there is a specific place where cooking happens, and there are ingredients that may or may not be available, but what the person who cooks does is to take part in a form of poiesis (a Greek word meaning formation/making) that happens contextually. These are not simply activities carried out by someone who wants to go against some kind of mainstream, but are everyday practices that are at the same time shared, that is, not necessarily individual, and particular, that is, happening in a specific context.

To explain these kinds of everyday practice, de Certeau employs the notion of 'tactic'. A tactic is fundamentally different from a strategy. It is a way of doing that does not try to exert control, nor is it connected to planning and overseeing knowledge. He describes it as the art of the weak, who use gaps in the system to act unexpectedly. When someone acts tactically, they take advantage of the circumstances they are in; they can engage in activities such as cooking and walking that are in fact micro-activities where they can be creative. Indeed, for a scholar like Michel de Certeau who 'proposed as a primary postulate the creative activity of those in the practice of the ordinary' (Giard 1998 p. XXXV), these tactics are key for the understanding of action in society.

Language is to be looked at in the context of the range of actions that individuals and groups perform. For de Certeau, focusing on language means looking at concrete ordinary practices which are in effect the locutory acts that one sees when examining everyday language. These are embedded in dynamics that involve hierarchies among groups and ways of using language, but show inventiveness and the ability to adapt (Certeau 2007, pp. 119–120). In *L'invention du quotidien*, drawing upon the work of J.L. Austin, de Certeau sheds light on the relevance of everyday language by emphasising its richness, logical complexity and its many connections accumulated over time. Not only is everyday language worth studying, but it is also less simple than one might think. When looking at idioms, for example, he sees 'a way to treat the language that has been received' (Certeau 1990, p. 43 my translation). In this sense, the kind of use de Certeau is interested in is not a production in itself (Pennycook 2010) but more re-use, again a way to 'treat' language. He also explains this concept by looking at proverbs: in proverbs, one can identify a form of representation handled by users. Telling proverbs implies a creative involvement on the side of the speaker in their being able to re-use them – rather than creating them from scratch – in a particular moment and in front of a specific interlocutor (Certeau 1990, pp. 36–40).

It is evident that de Certeau points us towards two kinds of action. One that has an overseeing character that is able to exert control. The other that is not based on full control but that can be creative thanks to forms of re-use. In the realm of language use, think of the writing of a novel, where the author, albeit using pre-existing linguistic/cultural forms, oversees the entire work; and think instead of the aforementioned telling of proverbs, where the ways in which things are said do not depend on an overseeing grasp on the part of the language user. The distinction between strategies and tactics, therefore, is one that relates to control over circumstances and doing, rather than power over others or lack thereof. The tactical nature of everyday practices is related to the eventuality of not necessarily having an overseeing knowledge of contextual elements, and yet being able to be creative. As Habermas (1986) would phrase it, it means to be able to engage in communicative action within the limits of the speakers' lifeworld. Another way to put it is that language use in the everyday can be described as an artistic tactic which involves adaptation to changes (Certeau 2007, p. 219). Speaking can be tactical in this sense; language is not simply given but includes the active involvement of the user, who does something while using language. Tactics are practices that involve moves that resemble those of a battle, while also being poetic and jubilatory: '[...]polymorphous manoeuvres and mobilities, jubilatory, poetic and military interventions' (Certeau et al. 1980, p. 8).

The re-use that for de Certeau is the basis of everyday language use can also be described as inhabiting (Certeau 1990, p. 51) and, in turn, inhabiting as a tactic (p. XLVIII). As for activities that have to do specifically with dwelling, one can consider the situation of a new migrant who finds a house in a new city. In this situation, the choice of where to live can be restricted as a consequence of the limited contractual power that migrants often have, at least at the beginning of their settlement in a new place. But the migrant can still do something creative. The limitations on a place to live in can be turned into something creative by superimposing one's own ways of inhabiting onto what is there. The migrants might not be able to leave, but they can use what is given in creative ways. The locale becomes a small-scale 'space of action, differentiation, experimentation and innovation' (Certeau 2007, p. 187, my translation).

Neither does using language imply a choice at all times. Something given, such as a language, can be inhabited; ways of using that do not fully belong to that language can be superimposed onto what is given. In this way, a language (or a place) can allow the speaker to introduce creativity into something that was not chosen, while remaining in it. These are ways of using, or rather re-using (Certeau 1990, p. 52), which multiply as ways to identify through a place become problematised by people's movement; and because of their lack of full control, in a way one can see speakers as renters rather than owners of their art (Certeau 1990, p. 111). Speakers would then be seen as those who do not have a wholesale control over their 'art', as de Certeau puts it, and yet are able to use it.

As de Certeau stressed on more than one occasion, these kinds of tactical moves have been growing in contemporary societies, in line with their detachment from traditional communities, also as a result of migration. Different things are gathered and used creatively in people's ordinary lives also when it comes to language. This use is consistent with multilingual language use, which, albeit not explicitly acknowledged in de Certeau's work, is clearly alluded to when he talks about language use precisely as related to processes of detachment from traditional communities. He was not assuming the exclusive presence of French when speaking about language in society, particularly if we think about the chunks of society he was looking at (often those at the margins), as well as his mentioning of migrants and movements in his metaphors and examples. In de Certeau's conception of everyday language use, then, there is a space of action – *un espace de jeu* (Certeau 1990, p. 51) – where the speakers can superimpose their ways onto what they have within the place where they find themselves. This does not mean transcending the place itself, but inhabiting it. It is more than dealing with restraints on grammatical and acceptability grounds (Gumperz 1964); it is about how meaning-making relates to concrete everyday circumstances, including those circumstances that are not chosen. As a result, the tactics that are linked to using language in everyday life are kinds of action where the actors seize the occasions that come up in order to be able to do something creative.

It is in the everyday that one can see the superimposition de Certeau is referring to and how it is involved in the use of limits to do something inventive. It is something beyond repetitiveness and yet strictly linked to re-use. These are 'unpredictable manipulations' (Certeau et al. 1980, p. 9) that are based on the ability to be creative within a given system. Something other than planned strategic action is connected to the ways in which orality comes into being and, in turn, 'the oral has a founding role in relation to the other' (Certeau & Giard 1998, p. 251). It is indeed important to reiterate that, while this kind of creativity can be realised by an individual's language use, it is something that happens because of an encounter with difference, meaning with someone else who is, therefore, an 'other'. To a sociolinguist, this brings to mind that 'language usage – i.e. what is said on a particular occasion, how it is phrased, and how it is coordinated with non-verbal signs – cannot simply be a matter of free individual choice' (Gumperz & Hymes 1972 p. VI). Drawing on scholars such as Sacks and Schegloff, de Certeau sees that there is a shared element that involves both what is used to communicate (the repertoire, we would say in contemporary linguistic terms) and how it is communicated, in that it implies the presence of another, an interlocutor who is part of the exchange.

Therefore, following de Certeau, we can focus on a speakers' space of action and their coming to terms with what they did not choose (Certeau 1990 pp. L–LI). It is within this space of action that creativity emerges, and its being able to introduce difference is predicated upon the acknowledgement that such a space of action is not boundless. As discussed earlier, instead of talking about mobility as if it were something available to everyone, de Certeau acknowledges that people do find themselves in places they did not choose and from where they cannot easily depart. This is evidently similar with a language. It is in this interplay between individuals finding themselves somewhere they did not necessarily choose (e.g. a language and a place) and their ability to inhabit it that de Certeau finds a way to describe what he finds remarkable. Speakers might be in a condition of having full control over circumstances and doing, but they can nonetheless be creative by using fragments of what they have at their disposal in the process of inhabiting.

In multilingualism research, there is much discussion around boundaries and 'whether and how poststructuralist interpretations of language adequately capture the ways in which multilinguals manage and navigate linguistic boundaries' (Jenks & Lee 2020, p. 221). De Certeau has repeatedly emphasised that language use in everyday life is immersed in a social setting where individuals experience limits and have to navigate them; we see practices that do not acquire any big role in society, but are disseminated. In fact, one can say that multilingual language use in everyday life becomes creative as it is bound by limits and, at the same time, can relate to these limits by adding elements that do not appear to fit within them. Boundaries themselves do not constitute a barrier to creativity. As one of the scholars who studied de Certeau's work extensively says, for him creative development grows at the margins (Di Cori 2001, p. 315). It follows that for de Certeau being creative is somehow different from counter-normative behaviour, in that it encompasses the very inhabiting of what is given. The existence of constraints emerges at the very root of de Certeau's view of how language use can be creative in everyday life. These constraints have to do with dealing with both linguistic and social elements that are not entirely chosen. It is in this tactical way of doing that one can find creativity, which for him is not incompatible with either re-use or the existence of a space of action which is not unlimited. This also includes linguistic practices that do not allow a speaker to gain any kind of strength or immediate social advancement, but that stem from a condition that actually allows for the active contribution of the speaker to get things done. Following this line of thought, one can see that as a speaker, one often makes meaning without trying to walk away from a condition that others may consider undesirable, while skilfully navigating one's linguistic circumstances with the intent of communicating something, making do with what one has. In this vein, I see the importance of seriously considering the material constraints migrants 'tackle in their daily dealings with circumstances' (Silva & Borba 2024, p. 788).

As Erickson (2004, p. 143) remarks when commenting on de Certeau's work '[...] we must consider the situated character of talk; the social action as a site of affordance as well as constraint upon local social action'. This reflection can help us visualise these practices while keeping the magnitude of what they do under the spotlight. Through de Certeau, we focus on practice not as a return to the individual (Pennycook 2010, p. 28), but as a sociolinguistic matter, taking an additional step 'away from the linguistic bias originally carried along in the discipline, and towards a sociolinguistics that attempts to understand society, not just language' (Blommaert 2013, p. 621). Gaining an enhanced awareness of constraints is not meant to limit or downplay the relevance of the creative endeavour that comes with multilingualism as an everyday practice, but to appreciate it for its own value. In this sense, it could be linked to asking whether and how a space of action contributes to the type of everyday creativity that research is interested in. In other words, casting light on these practices includes asking questions about their potentially lacking influence on a larger social scale (cf. Prinsloo & Krause 2019, for a similar point in educational settings). De Certeau did not arrive at the conclusion that individuals could use language disruptively to change their position in society, but showed that, in spite of the tremendous social constraints that individuals have to grapple with, a space of action is possible. The way in which de Certeau teaches us to look at these kinds of language practices is one that shows how the speakers can inhabit the weakness that is in their not being in full control of circumstances and doing. What de Certeau proposes is therefore different from a 'deliberate challenge' (Deumert 2018, p. 16), precisely because 'everyday creativity and expressivity does not need to imply disruption or transgression' (Deumert 2018, p. 16). He points to a tactical way of going about everyday life through language, which involves precisely the inhabiting of what is given.

Looking at multilingual language practices as creative in de Certeau's terms means first acknowledging that they can be seen as tactical, that is, practices that do not necessarily exert full control. De Certeau underlines what goes beyond that which is planned, repetitive and stable, in practices that take advantage of circumstances to be creative, but are not connected to a planning or overseeing knowledge. It also means acknowledging that these are dependent on a space of action. Inhabiting what is given for a multilingual can mean being in a position to do something unexpected, but it does not automatically imply engaging in an oppositional way with the unchosen. If we think about multilingual creativity as related to working through what is given to do something else, in some way, the whole realisation of the lack of full control on the part of a speaker can imply an ability to behave linguistically in a proactive way. This in no way should be mistaken for a way to couch multilingualism as a deficit. It is a way of emphasising the existence of alternative practices that potentially underscore the value of multilingualism in itself, in relation to the social dynamics in which it is involved.

## 2.2 Operationalising Constraints

Cognisant of these multiple voices and in a bid to go beyond the growing attention on repertoires as unfettered instruments for expression (Otheguy et al. 2015), the research presented in this Element explores language and migration by looking empirically at constraints among Gambians in Italy. Starting from a view of language practices within a space of action, as discussed earlier, I operationalise Michel de Certeau's notion of constraints as a lack of control over circumstances and doing (Santello 2022) concerning migrants' experiences by focusing on how these emerge as interviewer and interviewee build rapport (Goebel 2021b). Taking a step further from Dovchin's (2022) argument that forms of discrimination persist regardless of the celebration of playfulness of translingual practices, in this research, I pay attention to constraints as experienced by migrants. In other words, if 'it is apparent that transnational migrants are playfully involved with different types of transpractices, but it is not at all clear to what extent, how, and why particular local constraints either limit or expand one's translingual practices' (Dovchin 2022, p. 8), I open space for more experiences in a hitherto unexplored context, so that we can glean additional details on constraints among migrants. I am also mindful of what the author of the most extensive study of languaging and literacy in Gambia stated, in particular when highlighting the fact that '[...] speakers are always constrained by a variety of limitations [...]' (Juffermans 2015, p. 103). My focus here expands on de Certeau's (1990) view whereby creativity in everyday life often entails working within a space of action, thanks to tactics which involve having to make do with what is given. The notion of tactic again aligns with Michel de Certeau's view in the sense that, while strategies are actions that tend to have an overarching control over circumstances and doing, tactics operate within a space of action without full control.

It is the case of many migrants who do not have full control over many aspects of their lives, including where they live or the languages they can use to do things, and yet find creative ways to get things done. This type of view, rather than hinging on the notion of agency, which is traditionally seen in opposition to power and structure, focuses on what happens within a space of action. To put it differently, 'the distinction between strategies and tactics [...] is one that relates to control over circumstances and doing, rather than power over others or lack thereof' (Santello 2022, p. 686). I pay attention to constraints intended as lack of control over circumstances and doing 'as experienced by migrants, conceiving the possibility that they might function as something more than impediments to unbridled use' (Santello 2025b, p. 4). Although previous scholarship has not considered them as such, constraints can indeed be generative of possibilities (Canagarajah 2024). The focus here is therefore not on structures of power or how state politics influence certain processes such as learning Italian (Del Percio 2018), but zooms into the interactional level to understand how the experience of not being in full control of circumstances and doing is articulated between interviewer and interviewee with reference to language.

This research took place in a shelter for migrants in Padua, Italy. In the region, there have been instances of anti-immigration behaviour intertwined with language at different levels (Perrino 2015, 2018), but there are also several initiatives aimed at helping migrants in various ways, including linguistically (Helm & Dabre 2018). Padua has been nominated European capital of volunteering and, due also to the presence of a large university, hosts a substantial student population who actively contribute to activities to enhance social cohesion. It is important to note that, at a more general level, immigration has been a politically fraught issue in the country for years, where there have been oscillations between strong anti-immigration positions and various appeals to welcome migrants, particularly those who cross the Mediterranean (Jacquemet 2022).

I was introduced to this group of migrants by the people who work for an NGO I have been volunteering for. My positionality is partly one of an insider, in that I have given my time to the teaching of Italian to newcomers, including refugees from various parts of the world, within the NGO. I have known them since the end of 2021, and I do what they ask according to what is needed and depending on the time I have and where I am physically located. I have done one-to-one tutoring, small-group classes and helped train volunteers. When I taught classes, I did so mostly with young men who had just arrived in Italy, and I have met a few times with a Gambian who had asked for one-to-one support. I had never been to the shelter before this research project, and I had not met any of the participants, although they might have seen me at a New Year's party the NGO organised and that I attended some months before starting the research. When I started the project, the NGO workers recommended this specific shelter, explaining that some of these migrants were struggling with Italian and probably had a lot to say, as they had been in Italy for a while. Many of these were Gambians with whom I could speak English and Italian.

Three participants, here identified with pseudonyms, feature in this Element. The first is Lamin, who has been in Italy for over six years and, after various stints in the south and the centre of Italy, arrived in Padua a few months before I met him. He was doing the dishes when I introduced myself to the group in the shelter's kitchen. It became clear that he was interested in expressing his voice, particularly because he could do so in English. He was on a fixed-term residence permit and had been living at the shelter for six months with others, the large majority from West Africa. He was working on and off for a factory in a nearby town and, in the meantime, was taking some Italian classes from volunteers in the shelter itself. He speaks English, Mandinka, Wolof, Italian and some Swedish, a repertoire that has emerged progressively in interaction with me (Santello 2025b). The second is Mario, a young man also originally from Gambia, at the time of the interviews, had been in Padua, Italy, for about four months. He speaks English, Mandinka, Wolof, Fula, German and some Italian. His migration route encompasses three main stages: (1) his arrival in the south of Italy, where he stayed in migrant camps in Sicily and then moved autonomously to Apulia; (2) his relocation to Germany and settling there; and (3) his return to Italy after three years in Germany. His stay in Germany constantly emerges during our meetings, often with a clear sense that his return to Italy was not a happy move. The third is Omar, who comes from an ethnically mixed family and had been in Padua only a few months when I interviewed him, after spending some time in Italy and in another unidentified European country, before returning to Italy. Besides English, Italian, Mandinka and Wolof, he also speaks Fula and some French. He is relatively highly educated, having attended English-medium private schools in Gambia when he was younger.

One aspect that needs to be spelt out has to do with my personal investment of time and energy for migrants, who matter to me personally, which is the same drive that prompts me to conduct this type of research. A second related aspect concerns the way in which the participants might perceive me and my role. Our common knowledge of English and their being aware that I dedicate my free time to migrants and that I have been a migrant myself have created ground for our exchanges. The fact that we have both been exposed to different cultural settings may also be thought of as something that we have in common. Yet we are different in many important respects, including race, citizen rights, and education. In addition, while as a volunteer I have very limited decision-making, unequal positioning persists. As previously explained, I do not work for the NGO, but as a volunteer, I may be viewed partly as an insider; thus, the participants might not feel in a position to say everything they wish to say about their current situation. These aspects are bound to impact our exchanges, for instance, in discussing certain topics and to what extent. In the analysis, I try to account for such moments, with the understanding that differences remain and that my positionality affects the ways in which things are approached and presented. Nevertheless, I have tried to create rapport with them, intended not as something that pre-exists the fieldwork but as a processual phenomenon (Perrino 2021) and as 'rapport-in-talk' (Goebel 2021a, p. 37). In keeping with an ethnographic method that nurtures the participation of the researcher for the emergence of data about language and migration (De Fina & Tseng 2017) and, conceding that 'the meaning of other lives may remain opaque to the researcher' (Blackledge & Creese 2023, p. 23), I endeavoured to create rapport with them that grew through the interactions. For example, there have been moments where Lamin raised his epistemic authority – intended as the position of authority in terms of knowledge expressed in interaction – in a way that problematises pre-conceived asymmetries between me and him. There are also instances where both of our experiences as migrants are brought to light, thus making it possible for us to talk about difficult circumstances, or where we show alignment. I analysed the interactional data considering elements such as hesitations, repair, code-switching, and paralinguistic elements, drawing on sociolinguistic stance (Jaffe 2009; Lempert 2008). Stance-taking is conceived in interactional terms, in that a specific way of seeing a stance object emerges as speakers build on each other's turns. In particular, I give consideration to epistemic stance, meaning 'the linguistic expression of the state of the speaker's knowledge' (Kiesling 2022, p. 416). I also include the affordances of material ecologies in language exchanges (Canagarajah 2021), where space has 'considerable significance in meaning construction' (Canagarajah 2018, p. 50). Instead of thinking about it as agentive in itself, however, here I consider it in relation to what speakers do. This is also a way to account for the context of the production of these retellings (De Fina & Tseng 2017). The transcription conventions, in line with the Jefferson's transcription system, are provided in the Appendix; English is in normal font, Italian is in italics, and German is in small caps.

## 3 Unearthing Constraints among Multilingual Migrants

This section presents different types of language-related constraints and the ensuing tactics that can be traced in the data I collected among Gambian migrants in Italy. Here I identify four clusters of constraints, namely (1) lack of support; (2) limited interaction in the 'local' language; (3) immigration status in conjunction with life events; and (4) others' behaviour. I conclude with a subsection titled 'more than language-related constraints: other concerns and suffering' that leaves space for what has surfaced that does not directly invoke constraints per se, although it still relates to the experience of not being in full control of circumstances and doing. Altogether, this section is an attempt to group into clusters some aspects that have a level of internal consistency, with the understanding that there are overlaps, some of which can be seen in my work published elsewhere (Santello under review, forthcoming).[2]

## 3.1 Lack of Support

The first constraint that can be identified is the lack of support from institutions, as it emerges interactionally between Lamin and me. This is inhabited through two key tactics here, namely support from volunteers and personal efforts. When I interviewed him for the first time, he showed up with a notebook filled with Italian language exercises, which he had planned to show me during the interview. He does so in this first excerpt.

**Excerpt 1**

1  Lamin: Like right now you know:: we normally have you know *classe* every Thursday tomorrow
2  we have Italian *classe*
3  I: Aha
4  Lamin: You know with one eh:: with one woman from I don't know where she is from he=she is
5  also a voluntary [name of NGO] here
6  I: Ok
7  Lamin: So she will be here tomorrow you know for Italian *classe*
8  I: Humhum yeah yeah yeah sure is this [name of another volunteer] *o* no?
9  Lamin: [name of the volunteer]
10 I: [name of volunteer] I don't know [name of volunteer] ah [name of volunteer] ah yeah maybe *ah*
11 *no no* that's not what I'm talking about (.) ok I don't know
12 [name of volunteer]
13 So every week you know I normally have once in a week Italian class so it helping me=it is helping
14 me a lot yeah because as you can see all this
15 [he shows me his notebook filled with Italian language exercises and I start browsing it]
16 I: Is this your notebook? Ah that's cool
17 Lamin: Like the *verbi* you know *irregulare* verbs like *io gioco tu giochi lui gioca* something like
18 that <*cucinare*> <*potere*> <*dovere*> *dovere* so things like that you know I have a lot of:: notes here
19 [Keeps turning pages]
20 I: *Ciao* [to another person]
21 Lamin: It's a lot (3.0) it's a lot
22 [I look attentively at the notebook]

---

[2] This section is also based on my previous OA articles that have been alternately paraphrased, re-used with the same wording, revised and/or recombined for the purpose of this Element. These are Santello (2025a, 2025b, 2025c). Section 4 also draws on the same studies, although much of it has been written specifically for this Element.

23  I: That's cool
24  Lamin: Mmm (3.0) I'm learning gradually you know
25  I: Absolutely but (3.0) that's great
26  Lamin: Yeah because I even want to go to school but at the moment there's no space
27  I: There's no space for school? What do you <u>mean</u>?
28  Lamin: <u>Ah</u>:: because I've been calling them you know for me to do maybe the *A due*=*eh Anuno*
29  exam
30  I: For *italiano*?
31  Lamin: Yeah *italiano*
32  I: Ahah
33  Lamin: But they don't respond
34  I: Ok
35  Lamin: So maybe there's no space you know
36  I: There's no space?
37  Lamin: Yeah but in the future I'd love to do it
38  I: That'd be nice

In this excerpt, it is notable that improving Italian is characterised as an activity linked to taking Italian classes. Lamin specifically mentions a non-Italian volunteer who goes to the shelter for classes every Thursday. I, in turn, try to establish a link by suggesting who this volunteer might be, thus placing myself more explicitly as an insider among the volunteers of the NGO. He suddenly remembers the name, making me ponder whether I know her. He may know that, as part of my volunteering, I teach Italian to newly arrived migrants and thus wants to reinforce with me that he finds classes useful. These classes are mentioned through code-switching, matching their content (Italian language) and evoking the word *classe* in context (they are possibly being called *classe* when the classes are on).

The fragment is also important because it allows Lamin to show his notebook, which he had brought along when the interview started. The use of this object is significant; it shows that "a lot" (line 21) of work is being done. Not only can he flex verbs and name infinitives, but he also knows grammatical terms in Italian like *irregulare*, a morphologically Italian adjective that here keeps the sound /jʊ/, which comes from the English equivalent 'irregular'. His attempts to work on his Italian are significant and the results are visible. This is in line with the fact that he is aware of his good competence in written Italian, which he had mentioned to me in previous exchanges when he said that he was fine reading Italian in comparison to other migrants whose oral/aural skills do not match their proficiency in written Italian. This ability is displayed here thanks to his notebook, which is 'capable of communicating meaning' (Canagarajah 2021, p. 3) because of its use by Lamin.

However, his commitment to language learning is confronted with the constraints he experiences, which he reports in the following turns. The lack of available space for the local Italian language courses that prepare for the A1 exams is detrimental to his development as a speaker. He is unsure whether spaces are available; he tried calling them, but nobody replied. Lamin clearly understands the progression that is meant to happen (in line 28, he self-repairs from A2 to A1) and shows a willingness to do so (line 37). He is highly educated, having finished high school and continued studying afterwards, so he knows the value of education, and learning for him is also explicitly linked to class instruction. But he says that at the moment he does not have the opportunity to make progress through structured education outside the shelter. Lack of availability in language schools for migrants in Italy has been shown to happen elsewhere (Del Percio 2023). Here, one can touch the experience of constraints from a personal perspective: Lamin does not see any alternative other than relying exclusively on a one-hour-a-week class run by a volunteer for his language instruction. He also knows I am an educator and value language learning, so he assumes I will be struck by the educational deprivation he recounts. He is right; I indignantly elevate my pitch when asking for clarification (line 27), a specific interactional stance which is evaluative and emotional at the same time (Jaffe 2009).

In this excerpt, therefore, he makes apparent how the help from a volunteer and his commitment to studying Italian are visible. Nonetheless, there is a constraint, a lack of control over circumstances, that he experiences: people from the local school where Italian is taught and exams are sat have not responded to his phone calls. His situation of being a migrant who, after over six years in Italy, has problems conversing in Italian is linked to concrete constraints. The help from the NGO is appreciated (his self-repair from A2 to A1 also denotes awareness that he is not at a zero-level) and is a way to inhabit the constraints, but for now the lack of responsiveness from the local school is a problem for him. In other words, the constraint is inhabited within the space of action rather than erased altogether, while he remains hopeful that in the future he will be able to sit in one of those classes he has been trying to attend.

In the following excerpt, I ask Mario to elaborate on his life in Germany, where he moved after a first period in the south of Italy, as explained in the previous section. I doubted it was all rosy when he arrived there, particularly with the language. He starts speaking not only about his difficulties with German but also about the lack of instruction he experienced.

**Excerpt 2**

1   I: And and tell me how was it with German when you first arrived?
2   Mario: It was very difficult still now sometimes when I sit like I feel myself my God I can't speak
3   this language is very difficult but sometimes when I sit I feel happy about it and I can say little bit
4   some people told me=you can speak German you know I said no I'm not good °you know° but I'm

```
5  trying nowadays yeah but like the affection I have is about like the my first year in Germany was
6  boring all inside home nobody can teach you nobody can you cannot have time for one hour two
7  hours with somebody who can you know who can help you (.) of course I use like [name of online
8  video platform] °you know too° and but I can't do it alone
9  I: Of course and that was your first year in Germany
10 [...]
```

The stance Mario takes towards his first experiences with German vacillates between satisfaction with achieving good competence ("I feel happy about it") and his perception of falling short ("I'm not good"). What has occurred is brought to memory and presented as a stance object thanks to reported inner speech (Tannen 2007, p. 115), and presented as a current experience even though he is no longer in Germany (lines 2–5). He takes a negative stance towards his boredom and lack of help during his first year in lockdown ("my first year in Germany was boring"). He did study German but could improve only up to a certain point without external help: he used resources online to teach himself, but there was no possibility of someone spending time with him, which he exemplifies here as a one or two-hour class. We see the relevance of material ecologies (Canagarajah 2021), here characterised as insufficient to fill the absence of teachers. In other words, online tools were helpful but insufficient. To such a stance, I react with clear uptakes which I keep using throughout the excerpt, and with my "of course" (line 9) I align even more strongly with him (Du Bois 2007). In this excerpt, therefore, we find the articulation of the lack of support that he experienced during his first year in Germany, which is connected to slow progress in that very period. Therefore, while the constraint was inhabited concretely through tactics including self-learning, there is a clear indication that support was needed and not provided. Learning by himself is depicted as something difficult, precisely because he felt the need to have someone to help him, which he did not have at the beginning of his stay in Germany.

As the two excerpts above show, although some constraints have to do with structural problems, such as the dearth of available spaces in state-funded language schools, others also have to do with isolation more generally. This is further developed in the next section, which focuses on limited interaction in the 'local' language, where I use inverted commas to signal that 'local' is taken as an umbrella term instead of 'national language', which would exclude certain contexts where the most common language spoken by locals is not the national language. It is to be intended as used for convenience's sake. Particularly, it should not be interpreted as a term that excludes other languages, that is, languages migrants speak, by characterising them as non-local.

## 3.2 Limited Interaction in the 'Local' Language

In this section, I start with one of the first excerpts from my interviews with Lamin. We were sitting on the common room couch where the television was active. Before starting the interview, we switched the television off, but soon after, another guest switched it on again, and it was on until the end of the interview. I asked him to recount his migration experiences and how language came into play. He told me where he was from and what he did in Gambia before migrating. He then went on to talk about the difficult first years in Naples and then in Tuscany before arriving in Padua. After sharing my struggles with him, like having problems in taking a bus when travelling around Taiwan because of my not knowing Mandarin, I asked him about his experiences in Italy without speaking Italian. He had mentioned before that, when living around Naples, he did not have to use Italian because the fruit-picking jobs he had were so basic that they did not require much interaction in Italian. Here I ask him to tell me about more experiences.

**Excerpt 3**

1   I: But for example if you had to ask for information? You didn't? Or did you =or were you able to
2   make yourself understood?
3   Lamin: Yeah because normally you know (.) from the *cooperativa* you know we go straight to the::
4   place you know where we normally site for work so
5   I: Ahah
6   Lamin: So we don't normall=for me I don't I don't normally go out (.) °very often°
7   I: Ok so::
8   Lamin: Sometimes maybe *in Napoli centrale* you know maybe when you want to buy something
9   like African food you can go there you know you can go there you know
10  I: Ah ok and then you speak English or whatever with fellow Africans?
11  Lamin: Yeah because so man ... there are many Africans you know living around those areas so it's
12  easy for us to communicate with them
13  I: Ok
14  Lamin: People from Senegal you know I can communicate with them
15  I: Can you? In what way?
16  Lamin: Yeah yeah because we are borders
17  I: Ok?
18  Lamin: Senegal is a francophone country Gambia is a Anglophone country
19  I: Ahah
20  Lamin: We speak English Senegal speak French
21  I: But?
22  Lamin: But our local language you know are the same
23  I: Ok but you're talking about Mandinka the=the?
24  Lamin: Mandinka Senegal some speak Mandinka but their main=main native language local
25  language is Wolof
26  I: Wolof yeah
27  Lamin: Wolof yeah so I can speak Wolof very good Wolof
28  I: Ah ok you didn't mention that before you just men:: Mandinka but you didn't mention Wolof
29  Lamin: Yeah yeah
30  I: That's what I was puzzled about
31  Lamin: Mandinka is my you know that's my tribe language but I speak Wolof too

```
32  I: You didn't mention that that's why I'm saying because I know that in Senegal they speak Wolof
33     but I thought like you didn't say he speaks Wolof
34  Lamin: Yeah I speak Wolof
35  I: There you go yeah
36  Lamin: Hundred percent Wolof
37  I: Oh I see I see that's great yeah
38  Lamin: So::
39  I: So actually you speak several languages
40  Lamin: Yes yes yes I forget to tell you you know I speak Wolof too
41  I: That allows you to communicate with the people from Senegal
42  Lamin: Exactly
43  I: That's amazing that's great did it happened several times with you to meet with Senegal people?
44  Lamin: Yeah yeah many of them because you know Senegalese they have been here for so long
45  I: Ahah
46  Lamin: They have been in Italy for like many many years you know
47  I: Ahah
48  Lamin: There are living in Italy you know so there's many Senegalese you know around those areas
49     *Napoli::* even *Toscana* region you know there's a lot of Senegalese living
50     around *Prato Firenze*
51  I: Ahah yeah did=did you meet them also when you were in *Toscana*?
52  Lamin: Yeah yeah yeah yeah I have many Senegalese friends you know
```

At the beginning of the exchange, Lamin conveys that, when he was living in Naples, he did not use Italian much for public transport because his travelling was mostly commuting from where he was staying (the cooperative) to his work site. He speaks about going out (line 6), meaning engaging in activities outside home or work, and when uttering the words "very often" he pauses and lowers the tone of his voice. I perceive a hint of sadness in this retelling. Here, the constraint is the type of life he was living, which required little interaction with strangers and, consequently, little opportunity to speak Italian.

However, his tone changes when he recalls episodes where he went grocery shopping near Naples Central Station. He mentions African food, thus bringing in Africa as a whole (rather than Gambia), concerning the food he can get. In answer to this, I reinforce this link with Africans by saying "fellow Africans" and asking him to confirm whether he spoke with them in English, leaving some room for other possibilities with my "or whatever" (line 10). He elaborates on this connection with Africa, telling me about his conversations and friendships with people from Senegal. He mentions that it is easy to communicate with them because they are "borders" (line 16), referring to the geographical vicinity of his country and Senegal. Interactionally, this is prompted by his mentioning Africa as a place of origin (Schegloff 1997, p. 97) embedded in this telling and my re-launch in asking for more details.

In the following turns, he displays a level of meta-linguistic awareness that allows him to take an epistemic stance towards me (Kiesling 2022), that is, telling me about the linguistic differences between Gambia and Senegal. He first distinguishes them based on English versus French-speaking countries, using the words "anglophone" and "francophone" (line 18). He then casts these language-based distinctions in opposition with local languages that function as common languages in the interactions he is talking about, namely Wolof and partly Mandinka (cf. Omoniyi 2006). He gives importance particularly to Wolof for communication with Senegalese: because of the specific migrant communities in Italy (lines 44–52), what facilitates communication here is Wolof, which he speaks "hundred percent" (line 36). But he had forgotten to mention Wolof when I asked about the languages he knew at the beginning of our interview, which resonates with an earlier example where the repertoire of newly arrived Gambians in Sicily turned out to be richer than what he had initially reported (D'Agostino 2022). In Lamin's case, Wolof surfaces in this exchange and reveals its significance for this specific migration experience after my asking about constraints and him mentioning instances where he went out, thus partially breaking his isolation. Wolof was not salient at the beginning of the exchange, but it is now, in light of a discussion about its specific affordances, namely the possibility of grocery shopping in African stores around Naples central station and making Senegalese friends. His living situation, where he does not need to speak Italian, is also populated by instances of interactions with other Africans thanks to his competence in languages other than Italian.

Once again, the constraint is being in a situation that involves little interaction, which is something that other studies have characterised precisely as a constraint among migrants with particular reference to jobs that provide limited exposure to and use of the local language (Holm 2025). Here it is followed by Lamin talking about other languages, expressing epistemic authority, when explaining that in Senegal people speak Wolof, which indexes a change in interactional relations, that is, greater authority for him. I, in turn, raise my own epistemic authority by telling him that I knew that already, but that he had forgotten to mention that he speaks Wolof. I also show a positive stance by using a stance marker (line 37) and then following up with clarifications, thus achieving stance interactionally (cf. also Du Bois 2007). He explains that Mandinka is the language of his tribe, stating the importance of Mandinka for him and his people, while Wolof is the "main native" "local language" of Senegalese (lines 24–25). For him, these labels together are good descriptors in trying to convey the status of Wolof in Senegal. This labelling is discursively introduced by Lamin, who uses specific terms such as "local" and "native", attributing meaning to them in and for this exchange, with a non-local non-native like me. As I explain below, this dichotomy gives way to alignment towards the end of the excerpt, showing the development of rapport-in-talk.

In the following turn, he again raises his epistemic authority, this time on Senegalese migration to Italy, to the extent that he can mention cities where these communities have settled, using the Italian word *Firenze* instead of the English equivalent Florence. He talks specifically about the size of the community and their long-term settlement in the country. The surfacing of Wolof is to be connected to its use with the Senegalese, who are brought up here in relation to their presence as a migrant community in Italy. The repertoire, therefore, surfaces here beyond the speakerhood he introduced at the beginning of the interview. We notice an increase in the visibility of parts of the repertoire in this migration context, as recalled by Lamin. While he has difficulties remembering any experiences with Italian because of his scarce use of the language when in Naples, he refers to the multilingualism of West Africa as enabling him to do things and make friends. It is linguistically interwoven with code-switching that marks Lamin and I as people who have gotten to know these cities with their own Italian toponyms. This move helps to re-establish alignment in contrast to the local/non-local division in earlier turns, thus advancing the building of rapport in interaction (Goebel 2021a).

The description of the constraint of living a daily routine that does not lend itself to much interaction with strangers is intertwined with the surfacing of other interactions in African languages, as we show epistemic authority and build rapport-in-talk. This part of his repertoire surfaces when he calls to mind his "going out" outside his work commitments and is articulated with awareness of multilingual repertoires and shared knowledge of Italian places between me and him.

This is developed in the following excerpt, where I ask him to expand on how he communicates with different people:

**Excerpt 4**

1  Lamin: You know Italy is not like maybe sssss some other part of=some other countries (.) you know
2  like (.) Sweden Finland you know or maybe::: yeah (.) there you know if you cannot speak you know
3  Swedish maybe you know they wi … you know if you ask somebody whether they can speak English
4  you know he will tell you hundred percent I speak English
5  I: Humhum
6  Lamin: So those kind of places you know it was but in Italy you know Italian is very very important
7  to speak 'cause (.) without that you know it will be hard for you to communicate with lot lot of
8  people
9  I: Humhum humhum and I mean do you get a chance to speak with with other Italians or with other
10 people who speak Engli::sh or::? Tell me a bit about that because I'm interested in how you m=here
11 you have lots of Gambian people so you speak your language all the time I guess
12 Lamin: Yeah yeah
13 I: But ehm if you meet other people for example who are not from Gambia ah how do you
14 communicate with them? Do you use …
15 Lamin: Like blacks or?
16 I: Not necessarily
17 Lamin: Or Italians?
18 I: Or also other migrants anybody
19 Lamin: Yeah other migrants you know (.) maybe those from Senega::l *Costa d'Avoro* Mali (.) eh::

20   Burkina Faso (.) and where::: Guinea=Guinea Bissau and Guinea Conakry you know
21   I: Humhum
22   Lamin: 'Cause those people they can speak my language=Mandinka
23   I: Ok
24   Lamin: So:: we can communicate you know but like maybe [name of a housemate] it will be hard
25   for me because [name of a housemate] cannot speak English you know he can speak only French
26   and Italian so:: for [name of a housemate] you know I have to speak only Italian [chuckles] so
27   maybe I'll bro=broke it but sometime he will understand sometime if you don't understand maybe I
28   call someone to come and explain it to you
29   I: Ahah but with him you have to speak Italian
30   Lamin: Yeah Italian because he cannot speak English he can speak only French and his native
31   language
32   I: Ok ok and how ehm is it ok for you speaking Italian with=with people?
33   Lamin: Yeah because it is the only way I can improve my Italian by:: speaking you know (.) talking
34   with lot of Italian

Here Lamin makes apparent that the situation in Italy when it comes to English is different from other countries, specifically Sweden and Finland, as migrant-receiving countries where one can count on locals' ability to speak English. He is not only cognisant of different European countries where migrants can settle, but also of their different proficiency in English. He focuses on Finland and more so on Sweden, one of the European countries that have hosted the largest number of refugees in recent years. He connects migrants having less difficulty in communication with the locals ability to interact with migrants in English rather than in Swedish (cf. Salö 2014 for an overview of English in Sweden), thereby attributing to the sociolinguistic environment the power to make things smoother for migrants like him. In establishing this comparison, he intends to convey his difficulties in Italy, contrasting different levels of competence in English in Europe. In this discursive move, he therefore marks his competence in English as valuable elsewhere but not in Italy. Here, English is less valuable because of its local spread and ensuing usefulness (cf. Kubota & McKay 2009).

In the following turns, he reinforces another facet of his awareness of linguistic repertoires across countries, developing what emerged in the previous excerpt around Wolof. In lines 19–20, he enumerates a range of countries that allow for communication in Mandinka, once again explaining to me the use of languages in West Africa, in this case, precisely the language of his tribe, mentioned through a code-switched English-Italian sentence. Mandinka is a language that is spoken in a number of countries, and this allows for communicating between his tribe and others in West Africa. Considering specifically the Italian context, he distinguishes between speaking with other Africans, which he terms "blacks" and speaking with Italians (lines 15, 17), thus creating a dichotomy which is meta-discursively apparent (Gal 2018). I, in turn, expand the possibility beyond the dichotomy by using the 'general extender' (Kiesling 2009, p. 188) "anybody". Yet, he keeps speaking about his experience with

Africans and acknowledges that this easiness is not all-encompassing, particularly when communicating with housemates whose background repertoire does not match his, thus recognising that Italian is also used among Africans. In this case, he describes his tactic as two-fold. On one side, he communicates in Italian or broken Italian, as he appears to say in line 27; on the other, when this does not work, he uses help from others whose Italian is better, showing once more that 'the ability to communicate is not purely an individual accomplishment. It is a collaborative accomplishment in situations of local practice' (Canagarajah & Wurr 2011, p. 10). Notably, he does not bemoan that he has to speak Italian with other migrants but even welcomes it as an opportunity for improvement, otherwise lacking in daily life. Interacting with other Africans who do not have Mandinka, Wolof, or English in their repertoire is thus a real constraint for him in that he has no control over it, but it functions as a prompt for him to practise Italian, which he deems essential to his migration success.

This excerpt adds an important layer of signification to what emerged in the previous one. The speaking of English and other African languages is linked to affordances, but having to communicate with other people at the shelter is handled with Italian and help from others if a background language is not an option. The constraint of having to choose Italian for interactions with another person at the shelter is welcomed as a tactic to inhabit another constraint, that of linguistic and social distance from Italians, which impacts his fluency in the language. Migrants struggle to find 'interactional opportunities' (Piller et al. 2024, p. 122), and here we see how this is inhabited, having to make do with what one is given, using resources without full control over circumstances and doing. What is noteworthy here is that multilingualism itself is constrained by the limited overlap between the two interlocutors' repertoires (Lamin and his housemate, who speaks neither English, Mandinka, nor Wolof), but this makes multilingualism work in a direction that Lamin welcomes. In other words, here constrained multilingualism is an opportunity for linguistic development, which is a goal of Lamin's that he cannot entirely reach with other means, for example, by attending regular classes, as explained in the previous section. Constraints are implicated in the multilingualism Lamin engages with and possibly aspires to, one that includes Italian rather than excludes it because of the other constraints he faces, which are evident in excerpts 1 and 3.

### 3.3 Immigration Status in Conjunction with Life Events

In Mario's case, we see the relevance of his immigration status, which is a problem for him in Germany, in conjunction with his father's death in Gambia. As we read these excerpts, it is crucial to state that Italy is often the first port of entry for many migrants to Europe, including those who do not wish to migrate to Italy. According to a 26 June 2013 regulation of the European Parliament and of the Council, the so-called Dublin Regulation, if these migrants apply for international protection in Italy, they usually cannot move to another country but have to stay in Italy, sometimes for years, before being able to reach another destination in Europe (Regulation 604/2023). I did not ask Mario if this was his case, but he did arrive in Italy, stayed for some time, then moved to Germany, where he was happier, and then reluctantly moved back to Italy. Next is how he tells me about his move to Germany.

**Excerpt 5**

1   Mario: And then I moved to Germany
2   I: Then you moved to Germany?
3   Mario: Yeah in Germany I was there like in 2019 November 26 I re-remember the date I was in
4   Germany and then I think in January in February like CORONA and for the first year in Germany
5   like 2020 I can say little bit bo=is boring not a little bit just boring life=every time in the house you
6   know °no school no nothing° and then the following year 2021 I started going sch-school in
7   Germany DEUTSCH [German] yeah just like here we can say *A uno A due* [A one A two]
8   I: Umhum
9   Mario: And then I started doing school for like two years then my Italian *permesso di soggiorno*
10  [residence permit] when is expired then I try to come to renew my document and then I can fly
11  home visit family and come back too
12  I: Absolutely yeah so so when when did you come back from from Germany? Was it long ago?
13  Mario: Yeah just four months
14  I: Ah four months ago?
15  Mario: Yeah
16  I: Ah ok wow what a change two years we two years you were in Germany?
17  Mario: Yeah like since November 2019
18  I: Almost three wow that's that's long
19  Mario: I was doing school there no work just school there
20  I: Just school?
21  Mario: Yeah because I want to achieve my dream there but >it's a little bit tough it's not like
22  Italy=you know< Germany is different
23  I: Tell me about that because I don't know
24  Mario: About Germany?
25  I: Ahah so you tell me that I wanted to achieve my dream but it was difficult but you mean?
26  Mario: They don't allow not only me just for all of first like if you left Italy go to Germany you
27  don't have like opportunity to stay there unless when maybe like you need when you have ehm you
28  can say emergency to be operate or you have some damage here they can understand or if you have
29  like sickle cell like eye problem that you cannot solve in Italy you go you need help from the
30  Germans for those kind you can have the opportunity but when you left Italy like you can say Italy's
31  boring I don't have a good life in it and it's gonna be difficult for the Germans to take as a like as a
32  refugee immigrants you know they gonna send you out >they will drive you out every time you
33  gonna deport you in Italy or in your country you know<
34  I: Umhum
35  Mario: For me or so I am not lucky in German but I like the place the country because the time I
36  was there like you know my mentality I was growing up every day to learn a lot more than here you
37  know so it was like that

This extended excerpt starts with his migration to Germany, which is a specific event in time, recalled to the exact date (line 3). This is most likely because the arrival date was brought up for a visa application in Germany and/or in Italy and is here recalled thanks to memory and its mobility, using de Certeau's (1990) terms, and used interactionally. Personal relevance is evident in the stance taken towards his first year in lockdown. It was a slow, boring period where not much happened, conveyed through a self-initiated self-repair, as opposed to what happened after; the start of language school in Germany, explained to me through code-switching into Italian, referring to the local certifications which he is currently considering and that he assumes I am familiar with (line 7). His stance towards the first period in Germany takes a clear shape when he says "no school no nothing", where negativity emerges clearly as well as sadness through the lowering of his tone (line 6). This was a concrete constraint which he experienced as a privation.

In the following turns (from line 9) there is a chronological leap forward where two years of schooling are glossed over, and his move back to Italy is brought to the fore as a stance object. He speaks about his move back to Italy as a way to renew his "permesso di soggiorno" (residence permit) and then fly home, by which he means Gambia. Therefore, his move is a tactic connected to a future affordance: the possibility of flying home, which right now is possible only at the risk of losing his rights as a migrant in Europe. This is a prominent issue for him, and in this excerpt, he reinforces his condition of having to leave Germany, which interrupted his hopes of achieving his dream. His stance towards this event is conveyed through expressions such as "they gonna send you out" and "it was difficult"; the unforeseen (Certeau 1990) is marked clearly as unwanted, which is a response to my request to elaborate, which I utter through direct reporting (Tannen 2007), thus placing his voice at the centre (line 25). Mario's future is projected as broken because he does not fall into the categories of people who can stay in Germany: the categories that would allow him to remain in Germany are, as he explains, being sick (lines 28–29) or being in an emergency that one would not be able to handle in Italy (lines 27–28). He contrasts his stay in Italy and Germany starkly, taking two different stances towards the two periods and, in particular, describing his time in Italy as boring. This somehow resonates with experiences of waiting connected to 'boredom and frustration' described by Phipps (2019, p. 50) among people who are going through the immigration system in the UK, but is here explicitly brought up in contrast to another period, the one in Germany, which is characterised by education and growth.

Mario has probably shared these reflections with social workers and other people, and is here bringing to memory and articulating anew his stance towards his return to Italy, by saying "you can say Italy's boring I don't have a good life in it" (lines 30–31). There was a lack of control over circumstances, as de Certeau would say, which ultimately led to him having to move back to Italy where he did not have "a good life" (line 31). Here, he makes apparent that his time in Germany was devoted to building a better future, but he encountered toughness, again compared to Italy's unchallenging environment. In other words, his past experience in Italy of little personal and social advancement is told here as a condition he had to return to, thus interrupting his personal growth. His stance towards this return is conveyed through expressions such as "I'm not lucky". The constraints he experienced, uttered at a faster pace in lines 32–33, are connected with the unforeseen and are brought to memory in relation to thwarted future projections. The prospect of deportation is evidently something that is on his mind and that bothered him when he was in Germany, and that he inhabited by considering the steps and behaviour that were going to be more conducive to remaining in Germany. This did not suffice, however, as he had to return to Italy, which meant that he stopped the positive circle of learning and growing that he had managed to create in Germany, including learning and using German.

In the following excerpt, we see even more clearly how having an unresolved immigration status caused him distress, also considering a significant life event, which resulted in him taking the decision to go back to Italy. As I will discuss in the concluding section of the Element, moving back to Italy has repercussions on his experience of migration, which should stimulate a deeper reflection on the policies that engender such experiences.

**Excerpt 6**

1 Mario: But also my first year schooling it was very good (.) I was concentrate to learn but now apart
2 [unintelligible] started sending me letter letter you know BRIEF I don't know e-mail letter you send
3 somebody letter leave country within one week you know?
4 I: Umhum
5 Mario: And then I tried to appeal that case I take a lawyer paid a lawyer but he didn't apply appeal
6 my case you know but if that time the lawyer appealed my case maybe the German will say this boy
7 don't respect us you know you understand?
8 I: Umhum
9 Mario: Because they need something in time not out of time so I know that make my case difficult
10 to stay and living difficult in Germany and then every week like every month they would send me a
11 paper like you have to leave the country °yeah so°
12 I: So you decided to leave?
13 Mario: °So I decided to leave° I was decide to leave like ehm like my father died ehm passed away
14 pfff like five month ago
15 I: I'm sorry to hear that
16 Mario: I have no documents to go home so I decided to come Italy and plan here my future I learn a
17 lot from in Germany it's ok it's part of the future sometimes you have to let some parts go
18 I: I see I see what you mean well it must have been quite something to change country I mean to
19 move from from one country to another and then back
20 Mario: And back

In the first turn (lines 1–3), he adopts a positive stance towards his experience in the language school where he improved his German. He brings up again that he had decided to concentrate on his studies, but, in this case, he also mentions a hindrance, namely, the letters he started to receive. From what he is saying, these are likely to be letters from institutions ordering that he leave the country ("letter you send somebody letter leave country within one week" in lines 2–3). His experience with these letters is troublesome; the stance taken towards their receipt is negative, in that it is placed in opposition to concentrating on learning through the adversative conjunction "but" in "I was concentrate to learn but" in line 1. His attempt to ignore the letters was unsuccessful, and these letters bothered him to the extent that he lost the concentration he wanted to retain for his studies. He again brings my attention to his visa problem, framing it in chronological terms. His appeal did not go through in time, and in any case, his wait made his situation more complicated. In his saying "they need something in time not out of time" he means that his not applying early was decisive in his inability to fix his immigration status: the immigration department would have interpreted his lateness in applying as a lack of respect. Here he brings to memory the specific constraint of having an unresolved visa status and the unsuccessful tactic (a possible appeal) related to it.

What comes after is a pivotal moment, the recent death of his father. My understanding is that he could not fly home because his visa status would have made it difficult to return to Europe, and thus, he could not be with his family at such a difficult moment. This most likely made him realise that he could no longer be in an immigration limbo, because it would have meant that flying back home would have been out of the question in the future too. Here, two circumstances converge, namely the death of a parent and unresolved immigration status. His past traumatic experience, intertwined with time-sensitive issues, impacts his actions when considering future occurrences. In these, we can see clearly how the interaction between me and him is important for what is being said, particularly when he uses repetitions (Tannen 2007), thus showing that he aligns with my rewording and clarifications (lines 13 and 20), and when I display emotion in interaction (Du Bois & Kärkkäinen 2012) in line 15.

The relevance of uncontrolled life events for language has been shown to play a largely underestimated role in applied linguistics (Canagarajah 2022), and such relevance is evident here in the way Mario tells his moves between Italy and Germany over the years. It is embedded in the lived experiences of migration as these experiences are shaped by intersecting structural hurdles and emotional life events. What we can see here is how the immigration status in Germany is complicated by the upsetting arrival of letters that ordered him to leave the country, the absence of an appeal and the bereavement he suffered in the meantime. In other words, rather than being exclusively macro-structural power dynamics from above, here constraints are, on one side, blatantly linked to an immigration system that does not allow migrants to choose their destination country and, on the other, connected to the very personal experience of losing one's father and not being able to fly back to mourn him. Mario talks about planning (lines 16–17), relating it to the circumstance of not being able to stay in Germany and his consequent decision to return to Italy. Here, he takes a stance towards his learning in Germany as something he concretely achieved but had to leave behind. His resignation ("it's ok") is linked to a more general impersonal "you" that places his situation beyond his individual case, as part of what people "sometimes" must accept as part of life. Clearly, this has an impact on his daily communication, in that his move back to Italy means that he has had to go back to learning Italian, even though he has spent years away from the country investing in his German. Therefore, once again we see that his experience of constraints is influenced by concrete circumstances that are both personal and structural – his father's death and his immigration status – and are inhabited through his decision to return to Italy. He does not exercise full control over these circumstances and doing in that he had to let some parts go in spite of having learnt a lot in Germany (notice the modality used in line 17 when saying precisely "you have to let some parts go"). He, however, is open to the possibility of going elsewhere in the future, as evidenced elsewhere (Santello 2025a), evidently only when his immigration issues are solved.

## 3.4 Others' Behaviour

Mario brings to memory also the way in which people told him to speak German rather than English in Germany, something I have also witnessed myself in my life in Italy when speaking English with a refugee, when we were told "You're in Italy, speak Italian".

**Excerpt 7**

```
1  I: Okay and there (.) I mean tell me about the beginning you know you said German was very
2  difficult and ehm so you know because I'm just picturing you
3  Mario: Yeah
4  I: Where you know everything is new and you don't speak the language and how do you do?
5  Mario: I speak English [smiling]
6  I: Okay [smiling]
7  Mario: Yeah oh so I speak English when you tell me speak German when I speak English the=you
8  have to speak German you are in German speak German I said wow I don't speak German I just got
9  a bit last month or last week you know that's how is it you know I like
10 [laughter]
```

Here he mentions English smiling, which gives me the impression that he finds the answer to the question rather obvious, thereby achieving its perlucutory outcome (Lempert 2008). English was the language he used when his German was falling short. He brings up the fact that people told him to speak German when they heard him speaking English, to whom he replied that he had not been in Germany long enough to be able to speak German, thus taking a negative stance towards this remark. With constructed dialogue (Tannen 2007), he describes English as a patch to fill the temporary gap he had at the beginning, and we laugh at his ability to banter by telling people they have no grounds to rebuke him. This brings up an underlying tactic he had not brought up well until this point: speaking English at the beginning of his stay in Germany, which allowed him to inhabit what was given. His stance towards English is here one that acknowledges the usefulness of the language while positioning it chronologically as preliminary.

The negative stance he takes towards people's remarks that he should speak German in Germany is noteworthy. It is connected to the unfair expectation that he should speak German soon after his arrival in Germany, when his language competence was at the initial stages of development, and speaking English was an understandable tactic. He not only takes a negative stance towards this rebuke in this interaction with me, but also there and then by speaking back rather than keeping silent. He did so by explaining the circumstances that led him to speak English rather than German. In other words, to defend himself, he had to justify his language choice.

In the following excerpt, it is noticeable how learning words for Omar worked differently according to the different languages in his repertoire, particularly English and Italian.

**Excerpt 8**

1  I: Mmm do=do you still feel that sometimes you struggle to communicate with people?
2  Omar: In Italian?
3  I: Whatever
4  Omar: No I am feeling of
5  I: Ok
6  Omar: I don't think so in English maybe I communicate because sometimes for people their
7  vocabulary is higher than you
8  I: Humhum
9  Omar: Sometimes they speak big words if you know what I mean big words that you cannot
10  understand so you have to ask them again what they mean
11  I: Sure sure
12  Omar: Let me give an example you say big words like six pm like English you have to go to like
13  dictionary to that word what does it mean. Not in Italian in Italian when you speak big words that I
14  never heard of I ask you what does this mean so if you explain it to me I just take note and
15  remember that for next time
16  I: Wow that's that's something
17  Omar: Yeah
18  I: And in English you don't do that?
19  Omar: No in English I don't do that
20  (3.0)

```
21  I: Ok do you want to tell me why you don't do that in English?
22  Omar: I wouldn't say I know everything in English but I know words in English because:: I have
23  been to nursery from there to primary school so basically my education was all about money they
24  had to pay for me to get education
25  I: Mmm
26  Omar: From one step to another until I reach senior school and then I decided to come to Italy
27  I: I get it I get it so basically you are saying well my English is good enough I yeah::
28  Omar: Not that good enough but I can communicate.
```

This excerpt is interactionally complex. I start by asking him whether he still struggles to communicate, and opened the possibility to other languages simply because I did not want to restrict his answers. He replies by talking about his English, which surprises me. He says that sometimes people speak "big words" (line 9), and their vocabulary is higher than yours. I sense that he might be speaking about me, which makes me uncomfortable. I did not feel he had problems understanding my words during the interview, but he might have interpreted my "whatever" with an implicit questioning of his abilities in English. It is a case of rapport-in-talk beyond achieving smooth and unproblematic exchanges (Goebel 2021b).

This miscommunication allows for something worth noting, meaning the different dispositions between English and Italian when his lexicon appears lacking. For Italian, he would be happy to ask for the meaning of a word on the spot, which is an efficient way for him to learn, while for English, he would not do that. His speakerhood is influenced by the English-medium education he has received, which required financial effort from those who supported him as a child (lines 22–26). He gives me an example of a tactic he would adopt for English: remembering the word and looking it up, using dialogue as inner speech (Tannen 2007, p. 145) to convey the thinking process while looking up the word. In Italian, instead, he is ok admitting openly that he does not know a word and does not mind consulting the interlocutor for an explanation. Interestingly, he concludes his stance-taking downplaying his competence in English. He most likely hardly communicates in Italy with someone about complicated topics in English; thus, this conversation is salient for him in this regard. However, while politely not challenging me, he alludes to vocabulary. The silence that breaks this exchange is also indicative of my embarrassment. Nevertheless, it is a moment that made something emerge which otherwise would have remained hidden, showing again the productivity of rapport as interactionally achieved.

Here, therefore, we can see the two tactics of asking for the meaning of words and looking them up, which are used for two different languages, that is, Italian and English, respectively. Omar responds differently to others' linguistic behaviour, according to the languages involved; it is a way in which he enriches the lexical knowledge in both Italian and English. He concludes by taking an ambivalent stance towards his competence by saying "not that good" but also "I can communicate", thus indicating that in this exchange, he adopts a positive stance towards his communication skills but not so much towards his competence in the language overall.

In the following excerpt, I built on something he mentioned, that is, migrants in Italy have a particular way of speaking. I ask him if he uses this way of speaking, too. This leads to a recounting of an episode where he went to a CAF (an office where one receives administrative assistance for procedures with institutions) and was told to get help:

**Excerpt 9**

1  Omar: Sometimes I use it eh like ah last week I went like *CAF* I met like a old lady there so:: I was
2  trying to pronounce something but it was not that very correct like he asked me what kind of *partita*
3  *IVA* do you want? I told her that I don't know because I never opened *partita IVA* so:: she asked me
4  to bring someone who can speak Italian who knows about you know *partita IVA* >I was offended by
5  it< so I decided to refuse I told her that I don't know much about *partita IVA* but I would like for
6  you to help me to know what I w=what I have to do you know instead of calling someone to help
7  me speak about what I am trying to say I would be embarrassed to you know call someone to help
8  me
9  I: Absolutely
10 Omar: An Italian person or something
11 I: I get it hundred percent yeah absolutely it rem=I remember once it wasn't about language it
12 happened to me when I moved to England ehm at that time I had already spent four years in
13 Australia you know and then before then I was in=I think I was ok with English you know (.) but
14 then I remember I went to the bank you know the way they treated me::
15 Omar: Yeah
16 I: Ehm it was a bit like you know you are new to the country and I also had that kind of sense like
17 I'm not having this you know why are treating me this way I think I am perfectly able to do
18 Omar: To do
19 I: This so I think I understand what you are saying why you were just a bit uneasy about that
20 Omar: I think so
21 I: I get it I get it the point is that it wasn't so much your Italian you didn't know about the *partita*
22 *IVA*
23 Omar: <The *partita IVA* yeah>

Here Omar recounts through constructed dialogue (Tannen 2007) a recent episode where he refused to be told that he was incompetent in Italian when he simply did not know about the specific administrative procedure he had to undertake. He told the lady that instead of sending him away to look for help, he was demanding help from her. He mentions specifically that he did not want to ask for help from someone, also because he would feel embarrassed about it. We, therefore, see two different stances. On one side is the insistence on being assisted as a patron who needs advice on which procedure to follow, which is supposed to be articulated as a positive stance, but in this case is not because of the clerk's behaviour. On the other, he expressed a negative stance towards asking someone else, particularly an Italian, to accompany him to the office to get the paperwork sorted. With reference to the former, he specifically mentions that he was offended (lines 4–5) and ended up refusing the suggestion, and my impression is that he has not yet opened partita IVA (a type of VAT number). It is also worthwhile noting that he connects this to his way of speaking Italian to the lady (lines 1–2). Remember that this recount follows one where he was telling me that migrants speak differently among each other and that sometimes he speaks in the same way with Italians, too. It is possible that he regrets using a non-standard way of speaking, as it might have triggered the patronising and dismissive behaviour of the clerk he is recounting. In this case, we see that he inhabits the constraint by accepting assistance as a patron for the administrative task on the spot, while not accepting the 'suggestion' to go away to seek linguistic help and return to the office.

From an interactional perspective, it is striking that I keep silent during his recount, while I had shown uptake through nodding and other markers throughout the interview. I felt indignant at what happened to him and was simultaneously connecting it to my personal experience of vulnerability. I start telling him how I was treated at a bank when I had just moved to England and how unpleasant that was. He is listening carefully and showing uptake (lines 15 and 18). I usually tell my experience so that it helps build rapport-in-talk that allows for the experiences of migrants to surface, but here I told someone, perhaps for the first time, about that humiliating episode and how offended I felt at that time. The tables are turning. My experience of discrimination gets listened to, as shown by his 'collaborative completion', that is, when one speaker finishes a prior speaker's utterance (Gardner 2001, p. 2), and he is there to listen to it.

This episode at the office brings to mind what Baynham and Lee (2019, pp. 77–96) report when talking about migrants in Leeds, UK, having to access discourses when trying to do more technical tasks. Here, it is evident that what made Omar jump was that he could do everything in Italian but simply did not have the technical information for what he needed. This could have happened to an Italian the same way, but no Italian would have been told to go away and bring someone who could speak the language. It is, therefore, a form of language-based discrimination similar to those that Dovchin (2022) described. In this case, assumed language incompetence was used to dismiss a migrant's rightful request; trying to overcome the constraint here did not work even when cooperation was specifically requested (lines 5–8). Sometimes, "instead of making extra efforts to bridge language barriers, those who are linguistically privileged often prefer to close their ears – and hearts – to those they find difficult to understand" (Piller 2025, p. 77).

## 3.5 More than Language-Related Constraints: Other Concerns and Suffering

While waiting for his rice to be cooked on the stove, Lamin and I sat in the shelter corridor when I asked him whether he had thought about learning Italian when he migrated. He replied as follows:

**Excerpt 10**

```
1   Lamin: Ah for us you know that's not our::: you know that's not our main concern you know
2   I: Ahah
3   Lamin: Our main concern is you know maybe [chuckles] whether I will=whether I will break in
4   Italy or I will die on the road those the:: those are our main concern
5   I: Ahah
6   Lamin: Because it's a very dangerous you know road you know
7   I: Absolutely yeah
8   Lamin: After from Gambia [list of countries including an instance of self-repair] have to cross the
9   Mediterranean Sea you know to
10  [someone greets him and then someone else asks him to go check on his rice on the stove]
11  Lamin: So it's a long road you know
```

Here, Lamin brings my attention to the concerns that mattered most to him when he migrated. He clearly speaks in the plural "for us" and "our main concern" marking this journey as a collective one (line 1 and lines 3–4). This characterisation of collectiveness is a discursive device that reports something concrete: the migration route is undertaken by groups of migrants rather than an individual. The enumeration of countries resonates with the previous ones that had to do with the spread of Mandinka (the concrete list from excerpt 4), but, significantly, he self-repairs to trace the migration trajectory that brought him to cross several countries and then the Mediterranean. What could initially be a list of countries connected via language becomes the succession of countries that he had to cross in order to make his journey to Italy. The point of this list is to represent a long journey, developed country by country, which is also charged with greater emotional value. He stresses the dangerousness of that road, saying that arriving safely in Italy is the number one priority, and the rest comes after. This is not surprising, as arriving safely has been shown to be something that migrants crossing the Mediterranean communicate first (Jacquemet 2020, p. 137), but this is his own personal story of survival, not only a collective one. In other words, Lamin's view casts the experience of migrating as collective, but he also positions himself as a member of a community of migrants.

Lamin shifts my attention from language to the risky journey he had to embark on, making me move away from my focus on language to what he wants to communicate. It is an emotional topic. He chuckles and performs self-repetitions (Tannen 2007); he is someone who could have perished instead of having this exchange with me. I am glad that he mentioned it because it brings attention to something I had not asked about explicitly (his arrival by boat) but assumed had happened. This shift, possible thanks to our rapport, allows this to be conveyed, something which suddenly focuses his recount onto what is salient to him first, and now also for me. Interactionally, here I am taking up the role of the receiver, aligning fully by acknowledging what he is saying and agreeing with it; I receive whatever he is giving me in this very moment, trying to show respect for something that I can only take in, facing the irreducibility of experience that Rampton, Maybin, & Roberts (2015) refer to.

A similar shift in focus also happens in excerpt (6), where, after telling him that I am happy that he is sharing his experiences with me and that I hope to make sense of them, he says the following:

**Excerpt 11**

1  Lamin: It's not easy for lot of immigrants you know (.) lot of immigrants are:: suffering you know::
2  at the moment you know
3  I: They are::
4  Lamin: Some don't even have a place to sleep=like for us you know without [name of the NGO]
5  you know we don't even have a place to sleep
6  I: Yes
7  Lamin: You know yeah because
8  I: You're absolutely right there's plenty of people::
9  Lamin: Yeah so::
10 I: You're right you're right
11 Lamin: Without without their help you know:: we could have been in a serious situation you know
12 I: [name of the NGO] is great ah?
13 Lamin: YEAH YEAH YEAH they help lot of people

Here, he wants to convey explicitly that immigrants are suffering. The suffering he is evoking has to do with not having a place to sleep (lines 4–5), a situation he had experienced in Tuscany, where he had to sleep rough more than once, as he had told me in another instance: intertextuality is at play again. He knows he is better off now because of the NGO and wants me to know that he and his housemates are in a fortunate situation that other immigrants do not experience. They are in that "serious situation" (line 11) that he can avoid thanks to the help of the NGO, which we both explicitly commend at the end of the exchange. Once again, he uses the plural, indicating an experience shared by many (the use of "lot of" in lines 1 and 13) and by some (line 4); the suffering is framed as a shared experience of "immigrants" (after the Italian *immigrati*), and so is the help from the NGO, although to a different extent. My own participation in this exchange is noteworthy here: we are both involved with the NGO at different levels, and our affirmation stems from our experiences with the NGO and most likely the anticipation of each other's stance towards its work. It is an active act of alignment from my side that both acknowledges the problems faced by migrants in Italy and the help offered by the NGO. We can see in this excerpt, more than in any other, the strengthening of mutual alignment and rapport; I not only listen but also contribute to and reinforce what Lamin is saying, and he, in turn, repeats three times "yeah" raising his voice (cf. Goebel 2021a). The concrete constraint of being homeless is here evoked as connected to the past and, at the same time, to the present situation of others. Suffering thus becomes a relevant aspect that emerges in the interaction between me and Lamin; it emerges through language but is not about language, and yet it is something that he cares to convey and as such finds its place here. As I will discuss in the next and concluding section, studying constrained multilingualism also aims at an expansion of our understanding of migration. By including here this specific aspect of suffering I mean to do justice to what Lamin wanted to convey beyond language-related constraints. He wished to communicate the situation in which he and other migrants are, qualifying it as suffering. There is something that goes beyond language-related constraints that belongs fully to this and other migration experiences; suffering is upscaled so that it can be seen as a collective experience. The result is that it shifts our attention away from a focus on language, encompassing other sides of life that he wants to voice.

## 4 Significance of Constrained Multilingualism for the Understanding of Migration

Migrants are not people who live constraint-free. There are many aspects of their circumstances onto which they do not exercise full control, and in this Element I sought to bring to light some of these aspects for the purpose of explaining how they are implicated in their lives with particular reference to language use. In this concluding section, I will do something that is often done at the beginning of a book, that is, talk about the genesis of this line of research. In doing so, I follow the path marked by Warriner and Bigelow (2019a), who used methodological meta-commentaries to make research processes more visible when working with migrants. I will also deal, as it is more customary, with the significance and the implications of the main findings, dwelling on their relevance for the understanding of migration, and not only of multilingualism, as well as on what this focus adds to current intercultural communication research.

This interest in constraints arose from my reading of Michel de Certeau, which I undertook extensively a few years ago. De Certeau is a highly influential thinker in the humanities and social sciences and has contributed to shaping scholars' reflections for decades. Yet, his contribution to linguistics has been limited to some scattered insights, which is particularly surprising for anthropologically-informed linguistics, considering that, of all the thinkers of his time, de Certeau is one who was greatly influenced by the ethnography of speaking (Searle and Austin, for example). Chasing up virtually all the volumes by de Certeau, thanks also to a period where I could be in Italy surrounded by libraries that, all combined, gave me free access to these books, I soon realised that there was something significant that he could say about multilingualism. His interest in migration and the ways in which migrants are creative through a process of inhabiting is what struck me. This is exactly what many multilinguals, including myself, do. We find ways to express ourselves using what we have within the space of action we are in, often being creative through what we gather and transport, and bringing it to use where we are. In my own life as a supposedly 'privileged' foreigner in four countries (Norway, Canada, Australia and the UK), in addition to my native Italy, I found myself in situations I did not fully choose and that did not necessarily make me glad or at ease. For instance, a bank clerk treated me in a dismissive and disrespectful way in the UK because I was a foreigner, and in Norway, I was 'forced' to rent a car in Norwegian, although the person at the car rental could speak English, and I could mention many more.

When I first decided to explore the experience of language-related constraints among migrants, I wanted to do so with newly arrived migrants for two reasons. First, I thought it was fascinating to find out how constraints are inhabited at the very beginning of entering a sociolinguistic environment when skills in the local languages are limited. Second, at the time I was volunteering in Padua, teaching basic Italian to people who had just arrived in Italy. I had mentioned this general idea to some of them during a class break when they were asking about me, and they were really encouraging and willing to contribute even though I had not asked them to. However, I explained in Section 2 that the NGO I volunteered for suggested another focus, that is, working with migrants who have already spent years in Italy. Many of them were not able to speak Italian fluently, and the NGO workers were not sure why. In addition, they envisaged that they would have had a lot to say because they had spent a longer time in the country. The NGO workers suggested a particular shelter, where I met quite a few migrants from Gambia who became the centre of this research. They indeed had a lot to share; I listened to the need on the ground, as it were, and that bore fruit.

In the central section of this Element, I highlighted some of what we shared through our exchanges and how we did so. Together, we were able to unearth constraints alongside the tactics to inhabit them. For example, we found that Lamin's situation of not being able to speak Italian after years in Italy is linked to a concrete constraint, that is, not being able to attend regular classes due to a lack of spaces at the local school, which was inhabited through personal efforts and help from volunteers, while hopefully waiting for a space at the local school. Mario experienced a lack of support from teachers and inhabited it by watching online videos, but this is something that he was not happy with altogether, precisely because he could not do it alone, as he words it. We also heard that Lamin was lacking interaction because of his working conditions when he was living in the south of Italy, whereas when he happened to go out, he used his repertoire with other Africans, particularly with the Senegalese, thanks to his knowledge of Wolof. He also explained that because English is not widely spoken in Italy (or at least not as spread as in northern European countries), he needs to learn Italian, which he feels he is still behind on. Yet, his knowledge of Mandinka allows him to communicate with many people from West Africa, which means that he can communicate across different communities in Italy. Interestingly, with one of his housemates he does not share any language, which makes communication difficult. However, rather than wishing that this were not the case, he welcomes it as an opportunity to practice Italian, which is otherwise scarce in his daily life. If their exchanges become too difficult because of his Italian, such constraint is inhabited through linguistic cooperation, specifically by asking someone to be an interpreter.

We also heard Mario having to fix his immigration status by returning to Italy, while voicing the past and present constraints of staying in Italy rather than in Germany. In Germany, after a period of immobility due to the Covid pandemic, he was learning and growing, while in his recounts, Italy is characterised as a place where he cannot do so to the same extent. Returning to Italy is something that he did reluctantly, but, considering the space of action he had at his disposal, he returned nevertheless. Fixing his immigration status is an important aspect for him, because it is also connected to the possibility of visiting his family in Gambia, which he could not do when his father passed away. Therefore, there are several aspects that he does not exercise control over, which include some emotional life events that he inhabits with different tactics, some of which did not work, like appealing a decision in Germany, while others might, like returning to Italy precisely to fix his immigration status. Of relevance is indeed the unforeseen, an aspect that is linked to migrant's lives and that has repercussions on lived experience with language; in Mario's case, returning to Italy was not foreseen and is a move he made at a specific point in time, given the circumstances.

Mario explains that he spoke English in Germany, but people's reaction to this was not necessarily positive, in that he experienced rebukes from people based on what we know to be a one-language-one-country ideology, that is, that someone in Germany should speak German. He inhabited it by telling people on the spot that he had spent limited time in Germany and by endeavouring to learn German through hard work. Omar, instead, experienced the constraint of not knowing certain words, which he inhabited by asking for their meaning and trying to remember them. He also experienced language-based discrimination at an office, which triggered the sharing of my own vulnerability when I was a newly arrived migrant in England. He inhabited the constraint by speaking back to the clerk, demanding to be assisted as a patron and not to be sent away to look for an Italian to assist him with the language.

Another important element that rose from this work is what I termed 'more than language-related constraints'. In particular, the role of suffering, principally in Lamin's recounts, becomes a key component of what he wished to communicate and that I felt needed to feature in this Element. Suffering emerges as he tells his experience of homelessness, which he is happy he is no longer experiencing thanks to the NGO that is currently hosting him. There are concerns that go beyond language that he conveys, including arriving in Italy safe and sound, rather than dying along the way, as has happened to many. These recounts stunned and humbled me, which is something that emerges in interaction as we bring these things to the surface, building rapport-in-talk that is far from an ideal, smooth, and predictable succession of turns, in that the exchanges encompass instances where things do not go as expected.

This goes in the direction of considering non-language-related aspects when studying language and migration, in line with a long tradition in social sciences that has cast light on intersectionality, which recent applied linguistic scholarship is bringing up to understand prejudice (Dovchin 2025b). Focusing on constraints as experienced and told in interaction means also making room for something migrants explicitly mention and that might be excluded simply because it does not relate to language straightaway. In the case of suffering or sleeping rough, it is not so much a social category that is foregrounded, although clearly these categories are implicated, but the telling of concrete circumstances and the impact they have on someone's life. In other words, non-language-related aspects have to do with circumstances that are brought to the surface when migration experiences are told, also when the purpose is to focus on the relationship between language and migration. For this, research needs to open itself enough to accepting and incorporating experiences that do not involve language explicitly or only partly so (see in the following).

But what does this all mean for our understanding of migration? In many cases, migration means living a life in a new language (Piller et al. 2024) and undergoing changes onto which migrants do not always exercise full control. Understanding how the dearth of support is lived concretely sheds light on the experience of having a need and what it means when that need is not met. It also means understanding the tactics that are put in place to inhabit such a constraint, so that we realise that migrants, rather than being passive, resort to material affordances, personal efforts and help from volunteers. This does not mean that the constraint is overcome through these acts, but that something is done within a space of action. Nevertheless, there are consequences of not receiving support, which we want at the very least to be aware of when considering the complications of migration, and when we devise policies. In this direction, policymakers, educators, researchers, and parts of the civil society, including NGOs, could enter further into dialogue so that what can be done is actually done.

Understanding what it means to have limited interaction in the 'local' language means understanding the conditions that migrants face, such as the scarce opportunity they have to speak the language because of a given job or location, or to resort to English when needed. Moreover, it means understanding that speaking among people who do not share repertoires can also happen in a shelter, and that this can be inhabited through linguistic cooperation as well as endeavouring to speak the local language. For migrants, it is not conceivable to remove all obstacles to communication. Constraints are part and parcel of trying to communicate across languages and, because of this, a deeper understanding of them effectively becomes an entryway into migrants' interactional dynamics in a new sociolinguistic environment. It includes instances when they welcome constraints as opportunities to achieve linguistic objectives that they deem important for their migration and are lacking otherwise, like indeed concrete chances to speak Italian. In this sense, constraints and opportunities do not necessarily need to be placed at two opposite sides of a spectrum but can be considered as circumstances as experienced by migrants in their complexity. Even so, this in no way exempts decision-makers from addressing the linguistic isolation that migrants experience, for example, in facilitating the creation of an environment where migrants can find interactional opportunities or be able to use lingua francas such as English when possible.

Understanding what an unfixed immigration status can bring to someone's life, particularly in conjunction with important life events such as the death of a close family member, means gaining a full appreciation of what they face in the here and now when their immigration status affects them, but also how tactics can work out. For example, knowing what happens when someone has to return to Italy after creating a life (and a language competence) in Germany can make us understand better how challenging a constraint can be and also the tactic chosen to respond to it (a move back to a country one did not choose). In other words, reluctantly moving back to the first country of arrival does have considerable repercussions on language learning and use, as well as on the experience of migration more at large. We may want to consider how laws and regulations impact migrants and the consequences these have on their lives and, down the line, on the communities they live in. If we keep a focus on language, for instance, what can we understand of this type of movement back and forth between linguistic environments? For example, what linguistic resources best allow to inhabit constraints so that these movements – if they cannot be prevented – become manageable linguistically. There is still much to be discovered as to the effect of these constraints and life events on language practices, if we wish to 'refine and deepen our understanding of how language issues actually play out in people's lives and, in particular, how they intersect with all kinds of inequality' (Saraceni 2024, p. 185). It is a side of constrained multilingualism that warrants extensive multi-country exploration.

Understanding how other people's behaviour impacts the lived experience with language, which is an important aspect this Element has made apparent, means enhancing our understanding of the potential impact of our actions in societies where not only languages but also often people we are surrounded by change. It means considering what Canagarajah (2022) calls relational ethics, which is linked to specific dispositions towards speaking and behaving ethically with people who are new to a country, so that positive change can be initiated, continued and strengthened, in consideration that "the perceived speechlessness of the linguistic Other more often seems to invite dismissal, even cruelty, abuse and hatred than solidarity, compassion and kindness" (Piller 2025, p. 77). It also means understanding the tactics that migrants resort to when they encounter a type of behaviour that is unhelpful or even hurtful, or discriminatory. There are many ways in which transnational migrants are discriminated against, some of which are still being identified and explained (Dovchin 2022). Here we see how instances where one is challenged or told off because of their language use are inhabited so that one can both consider the type of behaviour that represents a challenge as well as how migrants respond. It does not necessarily mean seeing in their response a way to solve a situation, although this might be the case, but it definitely includes viewing the constraint for what it is in people's behaviour (including our own). Service providers would benefit from a greater understanding of these dynamics so that, for instance, they can examine a migrant's perception of being sent away to seek linguistic help and the possible repercussions in their lives, such as delaying or failing to obtain an important administrative document needed for work. Re-examining one's communication with migrants is key to the good functioning of intercultural communication, and service providers can often make a real difference as to what a migrant can accomplish in a new country. But this re-examination can also apply to individuals who are not involved in devising any big policy but can nonetheless contribute to migrants' wellbeing through their ordinary interactions. This is, in all likelihood, key to the relational ethics Canagarajah (2022) speaks about.

Finally, as mentioned earlier, understanding the presence of aspects that do not necessarily relate to constraints, such as danger and suffering, hopefully can render us more aware of migrant's lives, however partially this can happen through academic work. Understanding that people risk their lives when crossing the Mediterranean can help us to devise solutions so that this is not the case anymore, and knowing the suffering they go through could prompt us to further investigate the causes that lead to that suffering and decide to act upon them. In other words, we might want to consider listening more attentively to the recounting of migrants' experience, even when their direct relevance for constrained multilingualism is not readily apparent. I was pleasantly struck by the openness of the editors and reviewers of *Language in Society* when they did not ask me to remove the suffering component of one of my papers (Santello 2025b) even though that aspect did not strictly relate to language. On a similar note, let us keep in mind that multilingualism is one side of migration, not the entire picture, and, consequently, collaborative, interdisciplinary efforts can contribute to an understanding of migration as a whole. This again goes towards the direction of making room for aspects that do not immediately relate to language but that emerge when experiences of migration are shared in interaction, also when studies are meant to focus on language. This might well mean further investigating the extent to which constraints are language-related, for example, by adjusting and developing descriptions and groupings of constraints such as those presented in this Element.

This body of research speaks to the growing attention in intercultural communication research to issues of language and migration, as exemplified in the works of Phipps (2019), Ladegaard (2023), and Ganassin et al. (2024). Piller argues that "the main challenges of intercultural communication are the linguistic challenges of language learning, the discursive challenges of stereotyping, and the social challenges of inclusion and justice" (2025: IX). If so, then looking at multilingualism among migrants, such as people from Gambia holding an international protection residence permit, goes in the direction of expanding intercultural communication research along those lines. This Element shows that intercultural communication not only happens in relatively more 'privileged' settings, such as those of international students, for instance, but also among migrants who go through the experience of living in a shelter. It therefore invites future scholarship to examine more extensively issues around language and migration when studying how intercultural communication works out. For example, what are the constraints encountered by migrants as soon as they arrive in a new country and try to communicate? How are they inhabited through language-related tactics? How does their lived experience with language change over time? What additional repercussions of the lack of support, limited interaction and the other aspects highlighted earlier are recounted by migrants when asked about their migration experience in relation to language?

Overall, more research is needed in the future to understand the constraints and the tactics to inhabit them when it comes to migrants and their language acquisition and use. In addition, much more work is needed to understand how to transform the policy-oriented points above into concrete workable plans, which require both willingness and practical skills to be put to use. A dialogue between different stakeholders, including policy-makers, can well function as a fertile soil for this type of endeavour, when different people – including researchers – and institutions decide to operate together. Turning research into policy can be challenging, and once more, cooperative efforts are much needed if a concrete positive impact is to be generated.

In conclusion, it is clear that there are circumstances and doing that do not allow the exercise of full control, and acting as a multilingual does not mean that one can steer the wheel where one wishes at any given moment. In the life of a multilingual migrant, there are situations where one is immobile or stuck, with incompetence, for example. This does not mean that there is nothing to do; it is our job to understand how constraints constitute a space of action and how migrants inhabit a space of action to communicate and do things. It comes with an enhanced consideration of constraints that shape such a space of action, in a way that considers their persistence in people's lives and their contribution to multilingualism beyond a linear association between multilingualism and boundary transcendence. Sometimes when I talk about constrained multilingualism, I am asked if I am sufficiently taking into account people's agency, to which I always reply that in no way my data show that people are passive. In this work I did not use the dichotomy agency/structure as my interest goes beyond power dynamics alone, and de Certeau's understanding of everyday life helped me to expand things in a direction which is personal in addition to societal. But tactics are precisely ways of acting; it is the creativity of migrants' multilingualism and the reality of what they live and tell in interaction that interest me. Again, de Certeau taught us that, in spite of the tremendous social constraints that migrants frequently have to grapple with, a space of action is often there. My hope is that in this Element I managed to place migrants at the centre, so that we have a clearer perspective on the constraints they experience and the ways in which multilingualism is intertwined with them.

# Appendix
## Transcription conventions

| | |
|---|---|
| plain text | English |
| italics | Italian |
| SMALL CAPS | German |
| ALL CAPS | louder speech |
| underlined | stress through amplitude or pitch |
| (.) | short pause |
| (3.0) | longer pause |
| [] | paralinguistic elements |
| () | translation |
| :: | phonemic lengthening |
| ° | soft tone or lower volume |
| ? | rising intonation |
| = | latch |
| > < | faster talk |
| < > | slower talk |

# References

Baynham, M., & Lee, T. K. (2019). *Translation and translanguaging*, Milton Park; New York: Routledge.

Blackledge, A., & Creese, A. (2017). Translanguaging and the body. *International Journal of Multilingualism*, **14**(3), 250–268.

Blackledge, A., & Creese, A. (2023). *Essays in linguistic ethnography: Ethics, aesthetics, encounters*, Bristol; Ingram: Multilingual Matters.

Blommaert, J. (2005). *Discourse: A Critical Introduction*, Cambridge: Cambridge University Press.

Blommaert, J. (2013). Writing as a sociolinguistic object. *Journal of Sociolinguistics*, **17**(4), 440–459.

Bonotti, M., & Willoughby, L. (2023). Linguistic prejudice and electoral discrimination: What can political theory learn from sociolinguistics? *Metaphilosophy*, **54**(5), 641–660.

Bucholtz, M., Casillas, D. I., & Lee, J. S. (2019). California Latinx Youth as Agents of Sociolinguistic Justice. In N. Avineri, Graham, Laura R., E. J. Johnson, R. Coley Riner, & J. Rosa, eds., *Language and Social Justice in Practice*, New York: Routledge, pp. 166–175.

Canagarajah, S. A. (2018). Translingual practice as spatial repertoires: Expanding the paradigm beyond structuralist orientations. *Applied Linguistics*, **39**(1), 31–54.

Canagarajah, S. A. (2021). Materializing narratives: The story behind the story. *System*, **102**(November 2021).

Canagarajah, S. A. (2022). *Language incompetence: Learning to communicate through cancer, disability, and anomalous embodiment*, Milton Park; New York: Routledge.

Canagarajah, S. A. (2023). A Decolonial Crip Linguistics. *Applied Linguistics*, **44**(1), 1–21.

Canagarajah, S. A. (2024). Crip translingualism: Boundary negotiations in (im)mobility. *AILA Review*, **37**(1), 54–78.

Canagarajah, S. A., & Wurr, A. (2011). Multilingual communication and language acquisition: New research directions. *The Reading Matrix*, **11**(1), 1–15.

Certeau, de M. (1990). *L'invention du quotidien. 1 Arts de faire*, Paris: Gallimard.

Certeau, de M. (2007). *La presa della parola e altri scritti politici*, Rome: Meltemi.

Certeau, de M., & Giard, L. (1998). A practical science of the singular. In L. Giard, ed., *The practice of everyday life: Volume 2: Living and cooking*, Minneapolis: University of Minnesota Press, pp. 251–256.

Certeau, de M., Jameson, F., & Lovitt, C. (1980). On the oppositional practices of everyday life. *Social Text*, **3**(1980), 3–43.

D'Agostino, M. (2022). Multilingual young African migrants: Between mobility and immobility. In A. D. Fina & G. Mazzaferro, eds., *Exploring (im)mobilities: Language practices, discourses and imageries*, Berlin: De Gruyter Mouton, pp. 17–37.

De Fina, A., & Mazzaferro, G. (eds.). (2022). Exploring (im)mobilities: Language practices, discourses and imageries, Berlin: De Gruyter Mouton.

De Fina, A., & Tseng, A. (2017). Narrative in the study of migrants. In S. A. Canagarajah, ed., *The Routledge Handbook of migration and language*, London; New York: Routledge, pp. 381–396.

Del Percio, A. (2018). Engineering commodifiable workers: Language, migration and the governmentality of the self. *Language Policy*, **17**(2), 239–259.

Del Percio, A. (2023). Speeding up, slowing down. Language, temporality and the constitution of migrant workers as labour force. *International Journal of Bilingual Education and Bilingualism*, **26**(10), 1197–1209.

Deumert, A. (2018). Mimesis and mimicry in language – Creativity and aesthetics as the performance of (dis-)semblances. *Language Sciences*, 2018 (65), 9–17.

Di Cori, P. (2001). Porte girvoli. A partire da 'L'invenzione del quotidiano'. In *L'invenzione del quotidiano*, Rome: Edizioni Lavoro, pp. 285–325.

Dovchin, S. (2022). *Translingual discrimination*, Cambridge: Cambridge University Press.

Dovchin, S. (2025a). Beyond translingual playfulness: Translingual precarity. *Language in Society*, **54**(4), 609–636.

Dovchin, S. (2025b). Beyond linguistic racism: Linguicism and intersectionality among Mongolian background postgraduate female students in Australia. Urban Education, 1–25. https://doi.org/10.1177/00420859251331555.

Dovchin, S., Oliver, R., & Li Wei (Eds.). (2024). *Translingual practices translingual practices playfulness and precariousness*, Cambridge: Cambridge University Press.

Du Bois, J. (2007). The stance triangle. In R. Englebretson, ed., *Stancetaking in discourse: Subjectivity, evaluation, interaction*, Amsterdam; Philadelphia: John Benjamins, pp. 139–182.

Du Bois, John W., & Kärkkäinen, Elise. (2012). Taking a stance on emotion: Affect, sequence, and intersubjectivity in dialogic interaction. *Text & Talk*, **32**(4), 433–451.

Erickson, F. (2004). *Talk and social theory: Ecologies of speaking and listening in everyday life*, Cambridge; Malden: Polity Press.

Gal, S. (2006). Migration, Minorities and Multilingualism: Language Ideologies in Europe. In C. Mar-Molinero & P. Stevenson, eds., *Language ideologies, policies and practices: Language and the future of Europe*, London: Palgrave Macmillan, pp. 13–27.

Gal, S. (2018). Discursive struggles about migration: A commentary. *Language & Communication*, **59**, 66–69.

Ganassin, S., Georgiou, A., Reynolds, J., & Ateek, M. (2024). Vulnerability and multilingualism in intercultural research with migrants: Developing an inclusive research practice. *Language and Intercultural Communication*, **24**(5), 385–393.

Gardner, R. (2001). *When listeners talk: Response tokens and listener stance*, Amsterdam; Philadelphia: John Benjamins.

Giard, L. (1998). Time and places. In *The practice of everyday life: Volume 2: Living and cooking*, Minneapolis: University of Minnesota Press, pp. xxxv–xlv.

Goebel, Z. (2021a). Rapport in the anthropological imagination. In Z. Goebel, ed., *Reimagining rapport*, Oxford: Oxford University Press, pp. 19–42.

Goebel, Z. (2021b). Reimagining rapport. In Z. Goebel, ed., *Reimagining rapport*, Oxford: Oxford University Press, pp. 1–18.

Gramling, D. (2021). *The invention of multilingualism*, Cambridge: Cambridge University Press.

Gumperz, J. J. (1964). Linguistic and social interaction in two communities. *American Anthropologist*, **66**(6/2), 137–153.

Gumperz, J. J., & Hymes, D. (1972). Preface. In J. J. Gumperz, D. Hymes, J. J. Gumperz, & D. Hymes, eds., *Directions in sociolinguistics: The ethnography of communication*, New York: Holt, Rinehart and Winston, p. V–VIII.

Habermas, J. (1986). *Teoria dell'agire comunicativo*, Vol. 2, Il Mulino: Bologna.

Harrison, G. (2013). 'Oh, you've got such a strong accent': Language identity intersecting with professional identity in the human services in Australia. *International Migration*, **51**(5), 192–204.

Helm, F., & Dabre, T. (2018). Engineering a 'contact zone' through translanguaging. *Language and Intercultural Communication*, **18**(1), 144–156.

Holm, A.-E. (2025). The situated nature of investment in language learning: The case of two new speakers of Faroese. In J. Simpson & S. Pöyhönen, eds., *Minority Language Learning for Adult Migrants in Europe*, Vol. 67–82, New York; Abingdon: Routledge, pp. 115–141.

Jacquemet, M. (2020). Transidioma afloat: Communication, power, and migration in the Mediterranean Sea. *History and Anthropology*, **31**(1), 123–146.

Jacquemet, M. (2022). From language to politics: Communication, power and migration in the central Mediterranean. In A. D. Fina & G. Mazzaferro, eds., *Exploring (im)mobilities: Language practices, discourses and imageries*, Berlin: De Gruyter Mouton, pp. 136–160.

Jaffe, A. (2009). Stance in Corsican school: Institutional and ideological orders and the production of bilingual subjects. In A. Jaffe, ed., *Stance: Sociolinguistic perspectives*, Oxford: Oxford University Press, pp. 119–145.

Jenks, C., & Lee, J. W. (2020). Translanguaging and world Englishes. *World Englishes*, **39**(2), 218–221.

Juffermans, K. (2015). *Local languaging, literacy and multilingualism in a West African society*, Bristol: Multilingual Matters.

Kiesling, S. F. (2009). Style as stance: Stance as explanation for patterns of sociolinguistic variation. In A. Jaffe, ed., *Stance: Sociolinguistic perspectives*, Oxford: Oxford University Press, pp. 171–194.

Kiesling, S. F. (2022). Stance and stancetaking. *Annual Review of Linguistics*, **8** (2022), 409–426.

Kubota, R., & McKay, S. (2009). Globalization and language learning in rural Japan: The role of English in the local linguistic ecology. *TESOL Quarterly*, **43**(4), 593–619.

Ladegaard, H. (2023). *Migrant workers' narratives of return: Alienation and identity transformations*, Milton Park; New York: Routledge.

Lempert, M. (2008). The poetics of stance: Text-metricality, epistemicity, interaction. *Language in Society*, **37**(4), 569–592.

Lippi-Green, R. (2012). *English with an accent: Language, ideology and discrimination in the United States*, 2nd ed., London: Routledge London.

May, S. (2022). Afterword: The multilingual turn, superdiversity and translanguaging – from heterodoxy to orthodoxy. In J. MacSwan, ed., *Multilingual perspectives on translanguaging*, Bristol; Jackson: Multilingual Matters, pp. 343–355.

Omoniyi, T. (2006). West African Englishes. In B. B. Kachru, Y. Kachru, & C. L. Nelson, eds., *The Handbook of world Englishes*, Malden; Oxford; Carlton: Blackwell Publishing, pp. 172–187.

Otheguy, R., Garcia, O., & Reid, W. (2015). Clarifying translanguaging and deconstructing named languages: A perspective from linguistics. *Applied Linguistics Review*, **6**(3), 281–307.

Pennycook, A. (2010). *Language as a local practice*, Milton Park; New York: Routledge.

Perrino, S. (2015). Performing extracomunitari: Mocking migrants in Veneto barzellette. *Language in Society*, **44**(2), 141–160.

Perrino, S. (2018). Exclusionary intimacies: Racialized language in Veneto, Northern Italy. *Language & Communication*, **59**, 28–41.

Perrino, S. (2021). Intimacy through time and space in fieldwork interviews. In Z. Goebel, ed., *Reimagining rapport*, Oxford: Oxford University Press, pp. 73–95.

Phipps, A. (2019). *Decolonising multilingualism: Struggles to decreate*, Bristol; Blue Ridge Summit: Multilingual Matters.

Piller, I. (2016). *Linguistic diversity and social justice*, Oxford: Oxford University Press.

Piller, I. (2025). *Intercultural communication: A critical introduction*, 3rd ed., Edinburgh: Edinburgh University Press.

Piller, I., Butorac, D., Farrell, E. et al. (2024). *Life in a new language*, Oxford: Oxford University Press.

Prinsloo, M. (2024). Fixity and fluidity in language and language education. *Journal of Multilingual and Multicultural Development*, **45**(3), 637–646.

Prinsloo, M., & Krause, L.-S. (2019). Translanguaging, place and complexity. *Language and Education*, **33**(2), 159–173.

Rampton, B., Maybin, J., & Roberts, C. (2015). Theory and method in linguistic ethnography. In J. Snell, S. Shaw, & F. Copland, eds., *Linguistic ethnography: Interdisciplinary explorations*, London: Palgrave Macmillan, pp. 14–50.

Regulation (EU) No 604/2013 of the European Parliament and of the Council of 26 June 2013 establishing the criteria and mechanisms for determining the Member State responsible for examining an application for international protection lodged in one of the Member States by a third-country national or a stateless person (recast) (604). https://eur-lex.europa.eu/eli/reg/2013/604/2013-06-29

Salö, L. (2014). Language ideology and shifting representations of linguistic threats: A Bourdieusian re-reading of the conceptual history of domain loss in Sweden's field of language planning. In A. Hultgren, F. Gegersen, & J. Thøgersen, eds., *English in Nordic universities: Ideologies and practices*, Amsterdam: John Benjamins, pp. 83–110.

Santello, M. (2022). Questioning translanguaging creativity through Michel de Certeau. *Language and Intercultural Communication*, **22**(6), 681–693.

Santello, M. (2025a). 'I said I'm young you know I can plan something good you know': Understanding language and migration through time. *Applied Linguistics*, **46**(3), 649–488.

Santello, M. (2025b). Constraints, suffering and surfacing repertoires among Gambian migrants in Italy. *Language in Society*, **54**(4): 683–705.

Santello, M. (2025c). 'No in English I don't do that': Exploring Gambian migrants' linguistic cooperation in Italy. *Applied Linguistics*, 1–20.

Santello, M. (forthcoming). Beyond textbook knowledge of the host country's language: Migrants' language-related tactics when not attending classes. In V. Tavares & S. Melo-Pfifer, eds., *Language Education and Learners of a Refugee Background*, Bern: Springer.

Santello, M. (under review). Migrants' future projections in conjunction with constraints. In P. A. Della Putta & E. Goria, eds., *Linguistic practices of migrants in and beyond Italy*, Berlin: De Gruyter Mouton.

Saraceni, M. (2024). Way forward: Down to earth with Unequal Englishes. In R. Tupas, ed., *Investigating unequal Englishes: Understanding, researching and analysing inequalities of the Englishes of the world*, Milton Park; New York: Routledge, pp. 182–187.

Schegloff, E. A. (1997). 'Narrative analysis' thirty years later. *Journal of Narrative and Life History*, **7**(1–4), 97–106.

Silva, D., & Borba, R. (2024). Sociolinguistics of hope: Language between the no-more and the not-yet. *Language in Society*, **53**(5), 775–790.

Silverstein, M. (2017). Standards, styles and signs of the social self. *Journal of the Anthropological Society of Oxford*, **9**(1), 134–164.

Tannen, D. (2007). *Talking voices: Repetition, dialogue, and imagery in conversational discourse*, 2nd ed., Cambridge: Cambridge University Press.

Tupas, R. (ed.). (2015). *Unequal Englishes: The politics of Englishes today*, London: Palgrave Macmillan.

Tupas, R. (ed.). (2024). *Investigating unequal Englishes: Understanding, researching and analysing inequalities of the Englishes of the world*, Milton Park; New York: Routledge.

Warriner, D. S., & Bigelow, M. (eds.). (2019a). *Critical reflections on research methods: Power and equity in complex multilingual contexts*, Bristol; Blue Ridge Summit: Multilingual Matters.

Warriner, D. S., Bigelow, M. (2019b). Introduction. In D. S. Warriner & M. Bigelow, eds., *Critical reflections on research methods: Power and equity in complex multilingual contexts*, Bristol; Blue Ridge Summit: Multilingual Matters, pp. 1–9.

# Cambridge Elements

# Intercultural Communication

## Will Baker
*University of Southampton*

Will Baker is Director of the Centre for Global Englishes and an Associate Professor of Applied Linguistics, University of Southampton. His research interests are Intercultural and Transcultural Communication, English as a Lingua Franca, English medium education, Intercultural education and ELT, and he has published and presented internationally in all these areas. Recent publications include: *Intercultural and Transcultural Awareness in Language Teaching (2022)*, co-author of *Transcultural Communication through Global Englishes (2021)*, co-editor of *The Routledge Handbook of English as a Lingua Franca (2018)*. He is also co-editor of the book series 'Developments in English as Lingua Franca'.

## Troy McConachy
*University of New South Wales, Australia*

Troy McConachy is Senior Lecturer in the School of Education at University of New South Wales. His work aims to make interdisciplinary connections between the fields of (language) education and intercultural communication, focusing particularly on the role of metapragmatic awareness in intercultural communication and intercultural learning. He has published articles in journals such as ELT Journal, Language Awareness, Intercultural Education, the Language Learning Journal, Journal of International and Intercultural Communication, Journal of Intercultural Communication Research, and others. His is author of the monograph *Developing Intercultural Perspectives on Language Use: Exploring Pragmatics and Culture in Foreign Language Learning* (Multilingual Matters), and he has co-edited *Teaching and Learning Second Language Pragmatics for Intercultural Understanding* (with Tony Liddicoat), and *Negotiating Intercultural Relations: Insights from Linguistics, Psychology, and Intercultural Education* (with Perry Hinton). He is also Founding Editor and former Editor-in-Chief (2017–2024) of the international journal Intercultural Communication Education (Castledown).

## Sonia Morán Panero
*University of Southampton*

Sonia Morán Panero is a Lecturer in Applied Linguistics at the University of Southampton. Her academic expertise is on the sociolinguistics of the use and learning of English for transcultural communication purposes. Her work has focused particularly on language ideologies around Spanish and English as global languages, English language policies and education in Spanish speaking settings and English medium instruction on global education. She has published on these areas through international knowledge dissemination platforms such as ELTJ, JELF, *The Routledge Handbook of English as a Lingua Franca* (2018) and the British Council.

### Editorial Board
Zhu Hua, *University of Birmingham*
Ali Abdi, *The University of British Columbia*
Tomokazu Ishikawa, *Tamagawa University*
Ron Darvin, *The University of British Columbia*
Anne Kankaanranta, *Aalto University*
Xiaodong Dai, *Shanghai Normal University*
Sender Dovchin, *Curtin University*
Phan Le Ha, *University of Hawaii and Universiti Brunei Darussalam*
Jose Aldemar Alvarez Valencia, *Universidad del Valle*

## About the Series
This series offers a mixture of key texts and innovative research publications from established and emerging scholars which represent the depth and diversity of current intercultural communication research and suggest new directions for the field.

# Cambridge Elements

## Intercultural Communication

### Elements in the Series

*Translingual Discrimination*
Sender Dovchin

*Short-Term Student Exchanges and Intercultural Learning*
Gareth Humphreys

*Intercultural Communication and Identity*
Ron Darvin and Tongle Sun

*Ethical Global Citizenship Education*
Emiliano Bosio

*Intercultural Communication in Virtual Exchange*
Francesca Helm

*Diversity, Equity, Inclusion and Intercultural Citizenship in Higher Education*
Irina Golubeva

*Constrained Multilingualism*
Marco Santello

A full series listing is available at: www.cambridge.org/EIIC

For EU product safety concerns, contact us at Calle de José Abascal, 56–1°, 28003 Madrid, Spain or eugpsr@cambridge.org.

www.ingramcontent.com/pod-product-compliance
Lightning Source LLC
LaVergne TN
LVHW011857060526
838200LV00054B/4391